Pathways
to
Success

First Steps for Becoming a
Christian in Action

from the author, as personal gift.
Nov. 5, 1998.

Pathways to Success

First Steps for Becoming a Christian in Action

by

Martin Mawyer

New Leaf Press

First printing: August 1994
Second printing: March 1995

ISBN: 0-89221-270-5
Library of Congress Catalog: 94-67320

Dedication

*To all those who had to bear
with me while I was learning the
principles in this book.*

Contents

1

Take the Journey

Turning points — every person's life has them. I can look back on my life and see dozens of turning points that changed my life, all for the better. I also realize that many, if not most, of those turning points could have changed my life for the worse.

Turning points can come unexpectedly, painfully, offering no hope, and be void of explanation. They can depress, confuse, weaken, humiliate, and cause great sacrifice. They can come unwelcome, without control, and lack all reason, logic, and belief.

I've experienced all these emotions, hardships, and struggles — and don't regret even one.

This doesn't mean I sit around waiting for another life-changing turning point to greet me. Like everyone else, I hate going through them. I suffer confusion, frustration, anxiety, and great sadness. Nevertheless, I understand the purpose of turning points because this is often the only way God can redirect us to the path He has chosen.

It is with this hope, this belief, and this trust that we all must turn and be pointed. Some of us must be turned and redirected more than others. But regardless of the number of turning points we must individually suffer, it is critical that we turn and discover where God is now pointing.

Here is a fact intrinsic in most turning points: We have no choice about the turning, but only we can choose whether to be pointed. We can choose to give up, become mired in our own sorrows, deny our own faith, blame others, and become hopeless, discouraged, or dejected. I have no question that God freely uses His great power to turn us, but it is only with our free will that we agree to be pointed.

Personally, I've probably gone through more difficult turning points than most — too many wrong paths, too many bad choices, too many environmental factors out of my control.

In February of 1973, I was in a military *mental* hospital from a drug overdose. I had no educational foundation, having barely completed high school. Of my 300 graduating classmates, I was in the bottom 25 academically. I was without any social graces. Our family was poor, rarely ever leaving the confines of our isolated backwoods home. A trip to the grocery store or to Grandmother's house was met with great excitement. A telephone didn't appear in the house for many years. Childhood friends never existed until my midteens, when housing developers finally built homes nearby. Even then, social contact was very infrequent. Being considered a social outcast, stories of the most embarrassing nature could be told of the physical abuse I suffered at school. It is not surprising, then, that my first job out of the mental hospital was as a janitor for a furniture store.

This is the cast of mis-shaped clay God had to mold to take me on my exciting journey through life.

God took a social misfit, uneducated in simple grammar, without any understanding of norms or even proper attire, a drug abuser, a former mental patient, a person who had held only a series of less-than-glamorous jobs, and turned me into a national spokesman, the president and founder of a multi-million dollar organization, an author, and a leading authority on religious and social issues.

From the wards of an insane asylum, God molded, shaped, and molded some more, so I could be placed in the presence of presidential candidates and noted politicians, quoted in all the nation's leading daily newspapers, thrust into national speaking engagements, and placed on television and radio programs — such as the "Larry King Show" — reaching millions of people worldwide.

Turning points — I've been through many. The incisions hurt, the castings seemed hopeless, the moldings came without warning, but through it all,

God was pointing. I followed.

I've learned much on my journey and I believe the experiences I lived can help many Christians reach that ultimate goal: living that special life which God created just for you.

More than anything, this examination is about principles. These principles work for everyone, not just myself. Some of these principles even work for the non-believing. Like gravity, they are laws which do not discriminate on the basis of religious belief. Because of this, these principles cannot be violated, ignored, or cast out. These principles demand hard work. They are not always understood, and they can cause temporary pain and suffering. But if followed, these principles bring success in every part of the journey.

Since the word success means different things to different people, I feel it is necessary to explain its meaning to me, especially its meaning to the point of this book. I believe God created each of us for a specific purpose: We are His workmanship to be crafted. Therefore, success, in this book, means *being where and what God wants you to be at every turning point of your life.* Now let me give a couple of words of caution: Sometimes you will feel successful and be an utter failure in the sight of God. Other times you will feel like an utter failure but be demonstrating great success to God.

How do we truly know whether we are enjoying success, despite feelings or tangible measurements? Simply by following God's overriding principles to success.

The journey is now yours to accept or reject. The

road is full of enjoyment and pain, fulfillment and frustration, happiness and sorrow. Once you start following these principles, the journey is no longer yours to control. Trust, faith, and hope are your only recourse in trying times. There will be many times when no one else can point the way for you, give you the right answers, or carry you on the road: It will solely be up to you and God. Others may be there to lend you moral and spiritual support, but ultimately the journey is yours and yours alone. You will find yourself praying for miracles, but the miracles you want will not come. You will find yourself praying for answers, but the answers you expect will never arrive. You will find yourself crying for help, but the help you crave will only drown in your own tears.

These words are not meant to frighten, they are a warning. Right now, God in heaven is constructing the next turning point in your life. It may be big, it may be small. But there's no question in my mind that God has already shaped the next turning point for your journey with Him. It may arrive soon, it may arrive much later. But it will arrive once you make that all important decision to be crafted into His workmanship.

Take the journey. It's the only chance you'll ever get.

Here's another warning: Simply reading this book will never put you on God's path to ultimate fulfillment. You must understand it, live it, remember it, and obey it. Many will nod their head as they read along. Some will enjoy the lessons and principles outlined. Others will even pass the book along or recommend it to their friends. Then, as is all too often the case, these people will deny its principles.

Which one are you? The doer or the reader? Personally, what matters to me is not how many people read this book, but how many people live the principles outlined. Despite popular myth, books rarely make people famous or wealthy. In fact, most authors are disgustingly poor and quite unknown. Therefore, there must be a stronger interest in spending the time to write it.

My interest is you.

2

No Excuses

You are the biggest obstacle to success. Only you can stop God's plan for your life. Others will not stop God. Circumstances and environment will not stop God. Money, intelligence, or good fortune have no hold over your destiny. It's not who you know, what you know, or what others know about you. That which is not within your control will never control God's plan for you. It's just you and God — not family, co-workers, employers, friends, government, pastors, or any other entity or non-entity.

If I had to point to a single reason why many Christians never experience the fullness of life it is: They all have an excuse — and not just one, but dozens of excuses. The real heartache is, these excuses are rooted in real events.

People have a weakness for excuses. They look for blame. They want an explanation for why they are failing or have failed. They want others to nod their head when told the terrible circumstances that prevent them from going on. It doesn't take much to find an excuse. Some are elaborate, others are simplistic, but, typically, all are real events.

The excuse, then, is used as a roadblock to prevent the Christian from walking down God's path for life. Sure, the person is still a good Christian, useful in many aspects to God, even enjoying life. But these people can never say, as Paul did to Timothy, "I have finished the course" (2 Tim. 4:7).

Through the course of journeying with God, you will be presented with hundreds of excuses as to why you can't go on. I've experienced most of these excuses. In fact, I would say there is hardly an excuse I've heard that I haven't also suffered. I will relate many of these personal experiences later.

Is there ever a legitimate excuse to use as a roadblock for following God's path? No. Can anything prevent you from finishing the course? Yes. YOU.

It is critical, then, for you to understand *you.*

"For we are His workmanship, created in Christ Jesus for good works, which God prepared beforehand, that we should walk in them" (Eph. 2:10).

In many ways you are unique from everybody else. In other ways you are the same.

You are unique in the fact that *before you were*

created God also created "good works" for you to perform. I find this simply exhilarating. I know, beyond doubt, that I was created for a reason. And the reason came *before* the creation. Let's touch on this for just a second. It's not that God created you and then debated about what to do with you, or how to use you, or where to put you. God had a specific job to be done on earth. Then He created YOU to do it. This is completely obvious even from human understanding. Businesses do not create products and then decide what they are good for. Henry Ford didn't create the automobile without a purpose. And God didn't create you without a purpose.

Do you remember God's very first command to man?

"Be fruitful and multiply, and fill the earth, and subdue it; and rule over the fish of the sea and over the birds of the sky, and over every living thing that moves on the earth" (Gen. 1:28).

I believe God had — and still has — many "good works" for earth. God in heaven, as Paul said, is creating good works. The only way God can send these good works to earth is to then create people for this specific purpose. The only way these people can come to earth is through birth. Therefore God said, "Be fruitful and multiply, and fill the earth. . . ."

Every human God creates is for this specific purpose: good works. Is it any wonder that Satan has abortion running rampant in all the world? Abortion is a direct assault against God's very first commandment to multiply, be fruitful, and fill the earth.

This commandment was so important that after God destroyed the world with the great Flood, it was His first commandment to Noah.

"Be fruitful and multiply, and fill the earth" (Gen. 9:1).

Envision God creating good works, then creating people to accomplish those specific good works, then sending them to earth through birth. This we know from Paul's Scripture. Now reflect on God's commandment to Adam and Noah to fill the earth. Quite obviously, God will not finish creating good works until the earth is filled.

When you were born, billions of people were already on this earth. Couldn't God find someone else to do these "good works" other than you? Perhaps so. But He chose YOU, created YOU, sent YOU to earth to do them. What possible good works could they be? Only God and you know. But if you don't "finish the course," you will never know.

Since Paul talked about life as being on a "course," it is appropriate that we think of our journey this way. God has placed us on a "course" for "good works" created "beforehand" in Christ Jesus. Since the "course" is *in* Christ Jesus, it is obvious that we must accept Jesus as our Saviour as the beginning of the course. We can't get onto the track without first finding ourselves in Christ Jesus. Until we do, we are just living life with no immediate, much less eternal, purpose. But once we do, we are then on the course for living the purpose God created.

The archnemesis of God, of course, is Satan.

Satan is running his course on the earth, God is running His. The ultimate battle, therefore, is earth. To give God the upper hand in this battle, YOU were created, before-hand, to do good works on earth. You were sent down from heaven above with all the skills, talents, and know-how to complete these good works. It is the job of Satan, once you arrive, to stop you. Satan's first step, obviously, is to keep you off the course: deny you Christ Jesus. If you don't accept the Lord Jesus, then you will never begin the course, much less complete it.

But Satan's war on you doesn't stop just because you accept the Lord Jesus Christ. Indeed, Satan suf-fered a loss (your soul for his kingdom) but that doesn't mean he is simply going to give you a free hand to work for God's kingdom. It is very important, then, for Satan to knock you off God's course.

The approaches Satan uses are varied and end-less. Here is where Satan uses your human nature which you can't escape.

As I said, you are both unique and the same. I touched upon your uniqueness. Before you were cre-ated, God had a job to be done on earth, then He created YOU to do it. But you were created human, with a sinful nature, placed on earth living under human restraints and conditions. You cannot deny your humanity. You are not an angelic being. You cannot create miracles on your own. You cannot move those who don't want to be moved. You cannot create wealth from thin air. You cannot choose the family you're born into, the environ-ment you grow up in, or your status, race, or nation at birth.

You have weaknesses and strengths, talents and handicaps, fears and hopes. You must work to earn a living, raise a family, be subject to environmental, business, or governmental actions.

In the end, Satan will attempt to use your humanity to knock you off God's course. Satan is not stupid, he will use real events to create real excuses to keep you from performing the "good works" which you were created to do.

Now please pay careful attention to these next words. God is generally the author of the real events which cause you temporary pain, hardship, struggle, and sorrow. Satan is the author of causing you to allow these incidents to be used as excuses for failing to complete the course.

There is nothing bad that happens to you that did not come from, or was not authorized by God for a specific purpose. That purpose is always to redirect you on the proper course.

Remember the story of Job. He is no different than you, and you are no different than Job. That's why God made sure the story of Job was included in the Bible. All the bad that happened to Job was authorized by God for a specific purpose. Job suffered greatly. He had every reason to blame God, Satan, circumstances, environment, friends, cohorts, and family. Keep in mind, also, that he struggled through the whole process; he was *not* perfect in all his responses; he was tempted, and fell to some degree — but in the end he kept his faith. God rewarded him greatly.

Whenever you think you have an excuse for

failure, remember Job. Whenever you don't understand why God is allowing you to suffer, remember Job. Whenever you think you have hit rock bottom, that the walls are caving in, that you are completely finished with God, remember Job.

It is important to comprehend that Job did not know why his world was crumbling. We have the benefit, when reading the story, of knowing the "behind the scenes" activity between God and Satan. Job knew none of this.

Job lost his family, his material possessions, his finances, his reputation, his dignity, his health, and more. He had friends who taunted him, accused him, and belittled him. Job had no Bible to lend spiritual support. Job had no Jesus Christ to offer spiritual strength.

Still, God expected Job to stay the course. And what a great course it was. For the "good works" Job was created for, and was rewarded mightily for, was a true life testimony for you and me.

After reading the story of Job, this message is crystal clear: NO EXCUSES. NO EXCUSES. NO EXCUSES.

3

Love Your Emotions

As humans, we are emotional beings. We feel sadness, happiness, and anger; ambition, desire, and drive; pain, sorrow, and suffering; joy, hope, and love; want, need, and cravings; contentment, peace, and satisfaction. The list is almost endless.

Though we may choose to ignore or change our emotional state, we can never turn our emotions off. Every waking moment is an emotional experience. Therefore, emotions tend to drive us toward pleasurable experiences while steering us away from all unpleasantness.

From childhood to adulthood, we train ourselves to gravitate toward pleasurable emotional experiences. We learn that emotions are necessary. We learn
that emotions, in and of themselves, are not bad, evil or
sinful. We learn that emotions are powerful, and at
times, uncontrollable. We learn that human life *is* an
emotional experience.

Whether conscious of the fact or not, all that we
do is subject to the emotional experiences we *want* to
feel. We eat because hunger brings sadness, want, and
pain. We play because entertainment brings relief,
diversion, and joy. We work because unemployment
brings dejection, hunger, and cold. We make friends
because friendship brings love, support, and compan-
ionship.

Even unpleasant activities fall under this rule of
thumb. We discipline our children, not because we want
to feel revenge, but because we want the love and joy of
raising respectable and responsible sons and daughters.

It wasn't by accident that God created mankind
with emotions. Furthermore, it is quite obvious that
emotions are not given to us for the sole purpose of
feeling good. Emotions enliven some, destroy others;
encourage some, enslave others; bring out the best in
some, the worst in others.

Christian or non-Christian, emotions dominate
our lives.

Emotions are God's gift to mankind — but this
doesn't mean all mankind is given the same emotional
pleasures or displeasures. Like fingerprints, we may all
have similar emotional imprints, but when examined

closely we are all different in our emotional experiences.

Now let's go back to Paul's Scripture in Ephesians.

"For we are His workmanship, created in Christ Jesus for good works, which God prepared beforehand, that we should walk in them" (Eph. 2:10).

If God created you for certain good works, and decided what those good works would be before He created you, then He didn't make any mistakes in your creation.

The emotions you were given are unique to you. Though these emotions serve many fine purposes, they are primarily there to help you perform the "good works" you were created to do. God gave you certain emotional desires, distastes, wants, needs, and joys to help guide you to those good works you were created to do.

Now this probably sounds obvious to some while repulsing others. I don't know how many times I've heard Christians say, "I don't want to do what I want, but what God wants." This may be honorable in its basic meaning. But taken to the extreme, Christians will never discover what God wants them to do.

God gave you emotional impulses to direct you to His chosen path. I don't want to make this sound overly complicated, because it's not, but I think many Christians have been afraid of their emotions. Somehow they believe emotions *are their own creation* and to follow them would be to do their will over God's. Well, you didn't create your emotions, God did. If you love science, it's not you who created that love for science. You are not the author of a single emotion in your body. God created that emotional love for science, not you. If you follow that love for science — as God designed it — you *are* following His will.

God gave you emotions which no one else in all the world — born or unborn — can experience. Because you are constantly in an emotional state, God gave you likes and dislikes to guide you along the path. In this sense, you cannot help but feel unfulfilled if you choose not to follow God's chosen course. That's because God doesn't want you to feel good about not completing the good works He created you to do. On the other hand, God wants to give you emotional fulfillment and reward for accomplishing the tasks He set before you.

It may be complicated to discover which emotional experiences are blessed by God and which are not and how to appropriately follow those emotions. But it is not complicated to understand that God uses emotions to direct, guide, and prod.

Let me use an illustration to make this point clear. God never said to himself, "I will create the apostle Paul, but I will deny the apostle Paul the emotion to want to preach the word." This would be cruel. God is not cruel.

But what did Paul say? "I am under compulsion; for woe is me if I do not preach the gospel" (1 Cor. 9:16).

Under *compulsion*. Compulsion is an emotional experience. God knew when He created Paul the good works he would do. One of those good works was to preach the gospel. Therefore, God gave Paul such an emotional desire to preach the gospel that he called it a "compulsion." Not only did Paul make it clear that he was compelled to preach, but added, "Woe is me if I do not preach the gospel."

This example is not special to Paul. God did not create doctors who hate doctoring, or mathematicians who hate math, or engineers who hate engineering. If they do hate these professions, they are on the wrong path indeed.

I respect what Christians are attempting to say when they state, "I don't want to do what I want, but what God wants." This is a great attitude to start on God's chosen path. But not everything you want to do is against God. In fact, that which God wants you to do is always in agreement with your emotions. Unfortunately, many Christians think that to pursue anything they like or enjoy is self-pleasure alone.

Nothing could be further from the truth. We are all called for good works and somewhere, in those emotions God created just for you, can be found what God has chosen you to do — and you're going to enjoy it, love it, and be thrilled by the experience.

This principle is necessary toward being successful in God: The answer to finding the good works you were chosen to do is found *within* you. Accept the fact that you are an emotional being. Accept the fact that God gave emotions unique to you for the sole purpose of guiding you along the chosen path. Accept the fact that if you are doing God's chosen works, then you will be the happiest, the most fulfilled, and experience the most joy and peace.

You are on a tremendously exciting adventure with God — and you don't have to deny your emotional loves, joys, and desires. In fact, you'll never find God's chosen path if you do. The rebuttal to the argument of those who say, "I don't want to do what I want, but what God wants," is "I am doing what I want, because *it is* what God wants, and woe to me if I do not do it."

4

Risk Your Talents

Emotions are just a part of the "good works" puzzle. You also have abilities, personality traits, intelligence, and aptitude as additional pieces. These additional pieces can be summed up as talents. Like emotions, talents are unique to you; and not only unique, they are God's gifts to you.

You may already be using some of these talents; others will be revealed at a later time. Whatever your talents, God will hold you accountable for their development, fine tuning, and use.

This parable by Christ to His disciples is revealing:

> For it is just like a man about to go

on a journey, who called his own slaves, and entrusted his possessions to them.

And to one he gave five talents, to another, two, and to another, one, each according to his own ability; and he went on a journey.

Immediately the one who had received the five talents went and traded with them, and gained five more talents.

In the same manner the one who had received the two talents gained two more.

But he who received the one talent went away and dug in the ground, and hid his master's money.

Now after a long time the master of those slaves came and settled accounts with them.

And the one who had received the five talents came up and brought five more talents, saying "Master, you entrusted five talents to me; see, I have gained five more talents."

His master said to him, "Well done, good and faithful slave; you were faithful with a few things, I will put you in charge of many things, enter into the joy of your master.

The one also who had received the two talents came up and said, "Master, you entrusted to me two talents; see, I have gained two more talents."

His master said to him, "Well done, good and faithful slave; you were faithful with a few things, I will put you in charge of many things; enter into the joy of your master."

And the one also who had received the one talent came up and said, "Master, I knew you to be a hard man, reaping where you did not sow, and gathering where you scattered no seed.

"And I was afraid, and went away and hid your talent in the ground; see, you have what is yours."

But his master answered and said to him, "You wicked, lazy slave, you knew that I reap where I did not sow, and gathered where I scattered no seed.

"Then you ought to have put my money in the bank, and on my arrival I would have received my money back with interest.

"Therefore take away the talent from him, and give it to the one who has the ten talents."

For to everyone who has shall more be given, and he shall have an abundance; but from the one who does not have, even what he does have shall be taken away.

And cast out the worthless slave

into the outer darkness; in that place there
shall be weeping and gnashing of teeth
(Matt. 25:15-30).

God is the Master. You and I are the slaves.
Clearly, God is using money (talents) as a symbol for all
that He has given us on earth.

God expects us to invest, even double, that
which He has given us. Furthermore, God is outraged
by those of us who simply bury God's talents.

Each of us have various talents. Talents are
turned into useful skills. For the wise investor, these
skills are constantly being developed, tuned, and used
for God's good works.

God put this Scripture in the Bible because He
knows that many Christians will be afraid to use their
talents. We fear failure and rejection. We dread taking
chances or putting our future at risk. The honorable
slaves who invested and even doubled their talents,
were clearly taking chances and risking their future. If
not, the third slave who refused to invest would not have
been afraid.

God knows all the assorted reasons for failing to
invest one's talents. He told the worthless slave that he
should have at least put the money in the bank to draw
interest.

Pride is the number one reason I see for failing
to invest one's talents. People simply do not like to be
criticized, corrected, or rebuffed when attempting to
use their talents. This is understandable. A person who
likes using a certain talent and knows that he or she is

good at this talent, is putting their ego on the line when rejection, correction, or criticism is met. They feel threatened, humiliated, and frustrated. Rather than risk someone shattering their talents to oblivion, they would rather keep it quiet — bury it.

God understands this fear (though He refuses to accept it) and says the person should at least put the talent in a bank to draw interest. In other words, if you don't want to fully risk your talents by setting out on your own, put it in the care of someone else or at least use the talent to a minimal degree.

My life can be used here as an example: God gave me a talent for writing. If I cower at using my writing skills out of fear editors would tear my writing apart, belittle my style, send me a barrage of rejection slips, and drive me into bankruptcy, I could at least write church bulletins and lower the risk. God would then get some interest from the talent He has given me.

A carpenter called by God to start his own construction business could at least use his craftsmanship as an employee of the business. A singer fearful of performing solo in front of large audiences could at least sing in a choir.

In fact, I learned that the best way to fully develop and multiply your talents is to at least draw interest on them.

This book, of course, does not encourage people to put their talents into a bank. This is a book about investing and taking risks with your talents.

Step number one in investing is to itemize your talents. You may not know all your strengths and weaknesses, these will be revealed as you journey. But you do know some of your talents and handicaps.

Write them down.

Make two lists. On one side, list what you like to do, what you are good at, and characteristics that are neither good nor bad. On the other side, list what you dislike or are bad at.

Be detailed. Paper and lead are cheap. Write them all down. Do not write down what profession you want to be in. You are only writing down talents: abilities, personality traits, intelligence, and aptitude. Also, these items do not have to be proven facts. Your honest opinion is all that counts here.

Let me give you a partial listing from my own list as an example:

GOOD AT OR LIKE
Writing
Communicating
Investigating
Debating
Public speaking
Comprehension
Determination
Patience
Music
Independence

BAD AT OR DISLIKE
Difficulty remembering details
Math

Can't keep a beat
Repetitive work
Schedules
Too many activities at once
Abstracts
Crowds
Public speaking
Doing what others want to do

Again, this is a partial listing. Notice that public speaking is on both lists. That's because though I believe I'm good at public speaking, I don't always like it.

Your list must be fair, ambitious, and all-inclusive. You will continually be adding, changing, and updating. Certain talents and handicaps will be revealed as you journey. For instance, it wasn't until I started doing media interviews that I learned of my handicap for extracting details.

This list on talents will be addressed again. But two points are critical here. First, your list is not an immediate guide to what God has called you to do. Look at your list as an inventory of ingredients — a wealth of resources that, when put together properly, makes a unique product. Second, the list of "BAD AT OR DISLIKE" does not mean God *will not* use these ingredients as part of your calling — in fact, He definitely will.

5

The Race Goes On

The purpose of being a Christian is not to be a clean, pure, golden vessel before God. The purpose is to complete the "good works" you were created to do. Being clean, pure, and golden is a part of the course, it's not the end of the course.

This is an extremely important point. Churches place great emphasis on ridding ourselves of sin. The apostle Paul spoke frequently about the vices that will keep us out of the kingdom of heaven. Jesus Christ said, "Therefore, you are to be perfect, as your heavenly Father is perfect" (Matt. 5:48).

Not surprisingly, Christians typically measure their spiritual progress on a sinometer (sin-o-meter) —

a gauge measuring spiritual perfection. At the bottom of the sinometer is a wretched sinner, at the top is a spiritual saint. Progress on the sinometer is determined by the absence of sin. One's usefulness to God is dependent on one's placement on the sinometer. God has no use for the wretched sinner, but great plans for the spiritual saint. Our goal, then, is to rise to the top — then God will use us.

At what point can God use us? At what point will He stop using us? At what point are we so righteous that God will open all doors? At what point are we so sinful that God will slam all the doors shut?

Refer to the sinometer — that's what many Christians do.

There are two problems outlined here: 1) Christians who believe their goal before God is only to become a clean, pure, and golden vessel. 2) Those who believe their usefulness to God is dependent on their sinfulness or saintliness. Both measure their progress on the sinometer.

Before I go on, I want to make one point extremely clear: God has commanded us to be perfect, pure, clean — a golden vessel. Nothing should be interpreted as a license to sin or demeaning the importance of spiritual perfection.

With this said, God does not wait until you are a perfect saint — or even close to such perfection — before He puts you on the course. You are immediately entered into the race as soon as you accept Jesus Christ as your Lord and Saviour. If you've done so, the course is before you.

Along the way, you will sin. You may even commit terrible, unthinkable sins. You may feel so low that you are looking up at carpet fibers. You may feel so useless that even entering into heaven will be stunning.

Big sins, little sins, medium-size sins — all sins tend to knock us off track, if not completely out of the race. Rare is the Christian who can pick him or herself up and begin running full force after sinning.

Early on it became clear to me why Satan works so hard to cause Christians to sin — to knock them out of the race, to keep them from finishing the course, to stop them from doing the good works God created them to do.

I set my mind to this one belief regarding sin: Sin will not take me out of the race, I will not take myself out of the race, Satan will not take me out of the race, only God will take me out the race. I don't care what the sin, how hard my kneecaps hurt, how clear it is to every other Christian that I am finished — until God shuts down the course, the race is still on.

If the sin is significant enough, Satan will always tell you the course is finished. You are then left picking up the pieces, putting your life back together, and then deciding whether God will allow you to go on or not. When this happens, read the story of King David. If ever God had reason to dethrone a king, it was David. Surely, in all your sin, you did not commit adultery and then send the spouse off to get killed, as did King David.

King David paid the consequences of his sin, as we will. But the consequences did not stop King David from completing his calling. Why? Because David repented, repented, and repented, every time he sinned. Repentance, that's the key to getting back on track with God and continuing the race. With repentance, God will put your sins as far as the East is from the West. He knows you are but flesh.

God has no purpose in knocking us off the course so we can run laps with Satan. God wants to reconcile us as quickly as possible. Don't demean the blood of Christ. You don't have to wait until tomorrow, next week, or next year. God is simply waiting for repentance.

Don't listen to Christians who so disparage your sin that they say you have to find another calling in God. Remember: "The gifts and calling of God are irrevocable" (Rom. 11:29). That's because before you were born, your good works were created. Therefore, they *are* irrevocable. You can't change them even if you wanted.

Pick yourself up, keep running.

Another critical attack against you by Satan is when you are going through turning points — those points in your life when all seems to have collapsed.

Here is when Satan is most cunning. You thought you were on track with God and then, beyond your control, all seems to come to a grinding halt. As a matter of fact, all the gains in your life seem to be going for naught.

Satan will then remind you of every horrible sin you've committed — no matter how long or short ago. We'll talk more about the purpose of turning points later. But right now I must dispel any beliefs, accusations, or assumptions that God is punishing you.

I've had Satan remind me of past sins, current sins, and assure me about future sins I'd be committing if I were allowed to go on. Unfortunately, these reminders sounded as though they were coming from God, not Satan.

Some years ago, I was fired from my job as editor of the *Moral Majority Report.* The organization had a new president who wanted his own editor, not one from a previous presidency. I had served as editor of the *Moral Majority Report* (the nation's largest conservative newspaper) for six years. I was also the author of a book, published by Crossways, called *Silent Shame: The Alarming Rise of Sexual Abuse.* Without question, I felt I was on God's race course and moving forward . . . until my firing.

I was not greatly disturbed at first. Certainly there had to be a purpose for my firing. God was moving me elsewhere. But the firing took place right before Thanksgiving. I had a wife, four children, a new home, a new van, and credit on some badly needed furniture. Thanksgiving came and went, as did Christmas. No job in sight.

Do you know what it's like being unemployed during this time of season with four children? Bills were coming in, funds were long gone, the future looked calamitous.

I prayed, but after a while the only words I heard were: "Martin, you can't go on. I can't trust you. You have failed Me in the past. If I allow you to go on, you will fail Me again. I have to stop you now."

And if not these words, then: "Martin, I'm punishing you for that sin you committed a few years ago."

"Why?" I would respond. "That was years ago, why now?"

"I allowed you to come this far because I wanted to hurt you more. Now you know how grievous you are in my sight."

And if not these words, then: "Martin, you are a sinner. When you clean up your life, I'll move you on."

At this point I had to ignore all logic, all reason, all feelings. I had to trust the forgiveness found in the Bible. I didn't feel forgiven. But even if I was forgiven, I wasn't sure this meant I could continue on in my calling. Perhaps my sin rendered me useless to God.

There was a time when I truly believed I was useless to God. Forgiven, yes. But useless nevertheless.

I explored my option: Go on with life as hundreds of millions do everyday throughout the world — on a course of personal fulfillment void of God. But soon I realized my heart would never let me. Still burning within my soul was a desire to go on, even if God seemingly wouldn't allow me. I had no choice. My heart could not be changed. I had to go on.

So I determined that only God would stop me . . . and He would have to keep stopping me because I would never give up. Couldn't, even if I wanted to.

I told God I know I'm a sinner. I probably will never be perfect, though I'll keep striving. I told Him I know that I'm a wretched soul. As far as I knew, I'd be a sinner the rest of my life. There would be no telling the type of sin I'd fall into, the embarrassment I'd cause, the disaster I'd set off. I offered no hope to God for reform, because I didn't know if I ever could reform.

I told God if He was going to hold sin against me, I should have never started on the course. He knew before I was placed on the course that I would sin. In fact, I asked God why, if He was going to hold sin permanently against us mere mortal humans, He ever created the course to begin with? We all sin. Sure some sin greater than others. Perhaps my sin is greater than others. But great enough to knock me off the course so that my only option was to run laps with Satan? Of course not.

I determined to pick myself up and go on. Suddenly this was logical, reasonable, and the only thing I felt like doing.

Shortly afterwards, a freelance job was offered to me. I couldn't see how it fit in with God's original calling of my life. Perhaps it did, but I was far from sure. Perhaps God had changed my destiny. Perhaps my destiny was changed because of my sin.

It didn't matter. All I wanted was a piece of God ... any calling was better than consigning myself to laps with Satan.

In hindsight, the turning point I suffered after my firing from Moral Majority had nothing to do with any past, present, or future sin. It was, as I first thought, simply God re-directing my life to fulfill my original calling.

Every sin is forgivable. Every repentance is accepted. Every calling is irrevocable.

I went to some length to bare my soul and reveal my thoughts because you, too, will be beset by sin on your journey. If God worked with only perfect people — those registering spiritual saints on the sinometer — then God would not have *anyone* working for His kingdom.

As both a secular and religious reporter, I got to know many current leaders of religious America. None are perfect. None ever will be.

I am squarely planted in God's calling for my life. Never been happier, never been more fulfilled, never been more convinced of my destiny. I got here, not because I'm perfect, not because I never sinned, not because God can't find millions of Christians who are more perfect than I, but because I kept moving, wouldn't quit, burned for God's calling in my heart.

If you have sins, I have greater sins. You probably won't hear this from many Christians who are walking in God's calling, that's why I'm telling you.

Christian leaders, who we believe are walking tall and mightily before God, are afraid to admit their sins. Not because they don't want to, necessarily, but because Christians hold them to such a high and impossible standard that they couldn't admit their sins if they wanted to.

That is why this chapter is so important. Perhaps you view these leaders as saints. Perhaps you believe they have been able to walk in God's mighty calling because they are so pure, clean, and golden. Perhaps you expect it of them, or perhaps you believe it to be the case because you don't see any of their faults or sins.

If you hold this belief, get rid of it quickly. Neither you, nor they, are ever going to rise that high on the sinometer. In fact, get rid of that old sinometer.

These Christian leaders got where they are with many faults that would surely astound you. But they made it.

You have one calling, you have good works only you were created to do, and these are irrevocable.

Stop counting your current sins and holding them against yourself to keep from going on. Stop allowing Satan to remind you of past sins. Don't allow sins to crush you when God is taking you through a turning point in your life.

Let me quote just a part of Psalm 51 which King David wrote right after his sin with Bathsheba and his guilt against her husband, Uriah, were discovered:

> Behold, I was brought forth in iniquity, and in sin my mother conceived me.
>
> Behold, Thou dost desire truth in the innermost being, and in the hidden part Thou wilt make me know wisdom.
>
> Purify me with hyssop, and I shall be clean; wash me, and I shall be whiter than snow.
>
> Make me to hear joy and gladness, let my bones which Thou has broken rejoice.
>
> Hide Thy face from my sins, and blot out all my iniquities.

Create in me a clean heart, O God, and renew a steadfast spirit within me.

Do not cast me away from Thy presence, and do not take Thy Holy Spirit from me.

Restore to me the joy of Thy salvation, and sustain me with a willing spirit.

Then I will teach transgressors Thy ways, and sinners will be converted to Thee (Ps. 50:5-13).

God answered David according to his prayer. He did blot out David's transgressions and did put him back on track with his unique calling before God.

When your sins are greater than King David's, perhaps then you should worry.

Truly repent and then move on.

6

Falling Down, Getting Up

It's time now to begin to put the pieces of the puzzle together. God's puzzle, however, is not like the puzzle you purchase in a hobby shop — a normal puzzle at least gives you a picture of what is to be. In God's puzzle, you are just given the pieces.

The total picture of the good works you were called to do will remain a mystery for quite some time. God has given you hope, but you can't really see where you are going.

Here's the hope you have discovered so far: The good works you were called to do were created *before* you. These good works are irrevocable. God has created you specifically to do these good works, and has given you the talents to perform them and the emotions to enjoy them. Regardless of your failings or stumbling, God expects you to get off the ground and run the course. God knows you are but dust, but flesh, a sinner at birth, and has given you Jesus Christ for repentance. Repent and move on. There is nothing that can happen to you that was not authorized by God. Remember the story of Job. Calamity, both real and imagined, will strike. But God knows exactly what is happening. God not only expects you to continue in your calling during these tremendous turning points, but He probably brought these turning points in your life to redirect you. You have no excuses — absolutely no excuses — for failing to complete your calling. Finish the course.

Here is the beginning of hope: You are a special creature in God who, Paul says, was created to be "zealous for good deeds" (Titus 2:14). A zealot is someone who is eager, passionate, and fiery about doing something. A zealot has fervor and enthusiasm. A zealot is determined, driven, and devoted. Zeal is an emotion.

Like a stumbling infant trying to take his first steps, we have to start somewhere. God can't direct us if we don't move. If you're waiting for a miracle, a sign from heaven, or God to move mountains, and you're not taking any steps, you'll never get anywhere. God is not going to bring your calling to you, He's going to bring you to His calling.

Taking those first steps is not overly complicated — it's the ability to continue to stand on your feet that requires time. At first you may stumble frequently, but that will improve. As in real life, walking is a learned process that requires development and coordination. Once you learn to walk, however, the steps are performed without thought. But that doesn't mean unexpected circumstances — like ice, snow, staircases, or your kids' roller skates — won't cause you to ever stumble. Fortunately people are rarely left paralyzed from stumbling in God's calling. You simply pick yourself back up — shake off the pain, the embarrassment, the ridicule from others — and carry on.

Taking steps, of course, should lead to somewhere. Not to worry. When a baby takes his first steps, he or she is simply learning motor skills — developing his or her God-given talent to walk. After a while, the child is going places for a purpose.

By now, you should have made your list of abilities, likes, dislikes, and characteristics. Somewhere on that list are your first steps in walking in God's calling for you.

My recommendation to you is to go through your list and isolate the one talent which you have the most zeal to do, and then begin to develop that talent. Don't ignore or discard the other talents. In all likelihood, many of the other talents will be used to buttress the one talent bringing you the most zeal.

7

A Buried Dream

Even before I made my list, I knew the one talent which brought me the most zeal: writing. I loved to write. I just didn't have anything to say.

Before going on, let me give you some personal background which could be a lesson to you.

In the third grade I knew I wanted to be a writer. I was encouraged by my teachers who felt my skill in writing was exemplary. I not only loved to write, but I was told I was good at it. I was so encouraged by my teachers that I even used my writing skills for devious activity — when I turned in book reports, I made the entire book up. Yes, I was a blossoming writer who didn't like to read. So I would make up a title for a book, give it a Dewy Decimal number, make up an author and write a report about a nonexistent book . . . and would get "A's." Dishonorable, yes, but the only "A's" I would ever get in school.

My teachers encouraged me, even in elementary school, to go to college to be a journalist. I didn't even know what a journalist was, but it sounded good to me. I remember telling my parents that my teachers wanted me to go to college to be a writer. Neither of my parents had ever stepped foot on a college campus. My father made just enough money to feed and clothe us. I was barely passing any of my classes, hardly college material. Even if my parents had the money, which they didn't, this would be a tremendous waste of resources. Besides, I was told, you have to be rich to be a writer. What I needed to do, my parents advised, was to pass my classes, graduate, and get a government job, like my father. Stop being a dreamer. Get a job in government. There's security there. Besides, one day you'll be able to retire.

All dreams of being a writer died in elementary school. I replaced the dream with nothing.

Pass my classes, get a job, raise a family, then retire — this is what I thought life afforded me.

I worked as hard for this future as you might expect: I barely passed my classes. A "C" was met with great excitement and congratulations, a "D" was passing and all that was really necessary.

There was one incident that bears mentioning, however. In high school I took woodshop. I did very well. I was working with my hands, producing something I could see (nothing ever got produced learning history or math) and got decent grades.

The school, however, decided to shut woodshop down. (It figured that the only class I got a good grade in would be eliminated.)

I protested. I went to my school counselor, the vice principal, the principal himself. Along the way, I was told repeatedly that woodshop was being shut down due to lack of interest. Lack of interest? You've got to be kidding! For us bumbling students, this was the only interest we even had in coming to school. Take away woodshop and our grade point average would be so low we might forever be confined behind these school walls.

I started a one-man crusade to keep woodshop going. I not only liked it and got good grades, but it was my only passport for graduating. I started a petition drive. Classmates were signing on who, even if paid to be in woodshop, would never be in woodshop. But how was the administration to know?

I delivered scores of names to my school counselor, who then took them to the principal. A troublemaker? Or a hero? I didn't know. Such an effort on my part, a social recluse, was stunning even to myself.

The crusade worked. Woodshop was reinstated. The school administration was impressed. I breathed a sigh of relief — I would graduate.

Then the school officials called me to the high school office. Once again I was told I should go to college and, this time, learn to be a woodshop instructor. (They must have looked at my other grades.)

I brought this news home as well. What a laugh. I hated school. "D's" were my patented trademark. Get a job with government, I was told.

By the time I graduated, writing was a far-flung thought. I had no journalism classes. My spelling was atrocious, my grammar worse.

I did what most kids would do with such an auspicious future: I joined the military. Nice government job, secure, and a solid retirement plan.

8

Bewitched

I joined the army in 1971. It was during the Vietnam War and I was 18 years of age. During this period you could enlist in any division of the army you wanted. I chose Army Intelligence, better known as the Army Security Agency. You might gather that the word "intelligence" had nothing to do with personal intelligence, but rather gathering sensitive information about other countries.

Upon entering, you have to take aptitude tests. Fortunately for me, these tests measured intellectual capability, not intellectual progress. After taking the tests, I was told I should go to West Point, graduate, and become an officer. But there was a catch: four years of free college meant six years of active duty.

Was woodshop offered? I asked.

Once again, I was being prodded to go to college. No dice, I said. I barely graduated high school — bottom 25 academically in a 300 graduating class. Besides, a 10-year commitment was more security than I was looking for. As far as I knew, I might hate the three years of military life I had signed up for.

I went through basic training and was then placed in an army communications school. The program was top-secret. It involved learning sophisticated computer communications equipment.

My classes brought me to Augusta, Georgia. Life suddenly got very interesting.

I lived off-base in an apartment complex with a military buddy. Living off-base was against military policy while going through school, but we braved it anyway.

During our training, we met many young people in the apartment complex. It was the first time I lived anywhere close to people, so I was fascinated. I also moonlighted as a swimming pool guard for the complex. I met many people this way, young and old.

You have to remember that during the Vietnam War, drugs were running amuck in the United States. Young people had long hair and were living an open counter-culture lifestyle. I, of course, had very short hair and dressed according to military guidelines. It was not the fault of the young people in the apartment complex that they always suspected me of being some kind of narc — a narcotics informer.

I assured them over a period of time that I was a soldier and was forced to dress and look like I was beamed out of the 1950's. Since soldiers were not allowed to live off-base, many of these young people were ignorant of what military people looked like, even though the base was only a few miles away.

I got to know many people in the neighborhood very well. Oddly, I can't recall one young person who had a father living at home. They all came from broken families, living only with their mothers.

One such family changed the course of my life dramatically. First, let me say I never went to church, though I had accepted Christ as my Saviour several times — I simply mouthed the right words out of fear of going to hell. But I think it did get God's attention.

With this said, I met Kelly while supervising the swimming pool. At best, we were friends. As striking as she was, she was even stranger. Unlike most teenagers, she was distant, somehow in her own world, and wore black fingernail polish.

One weekend afternoon I went to her house to meet her mother. Mother, too, had black fingernail polish on. Furthermore, she wore an all-black outfit, had a solid black cat, and had the weirdest pictures on the wall I had ever witnessed. Dark, silhouette, spooky pictures. Something seemed awry.

So I asked her, "How come you and your daughter wear black fingernail polish, have an all-black cat, and have these spooky pictures on the wall?" My bottled-up journalism was spewing forth.

"I'm a witch," she replied.

I was stunned, never having met someone who called themselves a witch. I wasn't a religious man, knew nothing about the occult, and lived an extremely reclusive life. My vision of witches were of the Halloween type.

"Really?" I said.

"Yes, both my daughter and I are witches."

"Come on, you're kidding me."

"No, I can prove it."

She led me to an end table which had a rather thick book on it. The author was America's "great white witch" at the time. I will not repeat her name, though this particular woman had been the subject of many legitimate news programs. This corresponded to the media's incredible fascination with the occult during the early seventies. The media's interest was spurred by the growing number of people entering the occult as a result of high drug use at the time.

Still, at that time, I had never heard of America's so-called "great white witch." The lady picked the book up off the end table and began reading aloud a handwritten note on the inside flap of the book. The note started out "To my loving daughter," et cetera, and was signed, "Mom."

"This is my mother," she said, assuming I had heard of this great white witch before. (Perhaps so, if her mother's name was Elizabeth Montgomery, and her name was Tabitha.)

I was unimpressed. This lady was wacky. I sat on her couch, she joined me at the other end. Behind her was her daughter, Kelly, sitting on a bar stool. We all sat in dead silence. She was awaiting my response. Certainly, she must have thought I was awestruck, groping for words, even stunned at this chance meeting.

I said what anyone of my character would have said, "So, do you ride brooms?"

My levity was not well taken. To this day, I have never again witnessed the evil look that I saw on her face. The silence was so thick I almost suffocated.

Then, after some time of eyeball-to-eyeball staring, she spoke, "Okay, let's do it."

"Do what?" I responded.

"My daughter and I were talking. . . ."

"Wait a minute. You and your daughter were *not* talking. She's sitting five feet behind you. You never opened your mouth."

"We were using mental telepathy."

Great, I thought, *not only is she a voodoo, cast-spelling witch, she's a mind reader to boot.*

"And what did you two talk about?"

"We decided to prove to you we are witches."

"And how are you going to prove to me you are a witch?"

"We decided to cast a two-week bad luck spell on you. The bad luck will get increasingly worse. If, at the end of the two weeks, you don't agree that we are witches, we will hold a doll of you over flames and burn you to death."

"Would you like to admit now that we are witches?"

Call it pride, call it ignorance, call it whatever you choose. "No," I said. (Somehow I wanted to be back in woodshop making a 12-inch wooden stake.)

"In two weeks you will." She sounded chillingly confident.

Over the period of the next *week*, not two weeks, many events happened, most of them developing concurrently.

First, a civilian friend and I went with his mother to see her brother. While at her brother's house, she got plastered on alcohol . . . and insisted on driving home. I had never ridden with a drunk before. Neither my friend nor I had ever driven a car before, much less had a driver's license. We were at the total mercy of his mother getting us home. When she started driving on the wrong side of a four-lane highway, I felt suddenly bewitched.

She asked if we wanted to stop and eat. No college degree needed here. "Yes!" we responded. While in the restaurant I excused myself to go to the rest room. Instead I went out to her 8-cylinder, gas-guzzling Ford Galaxy and pulled *one* spark plug wire from the engine. Those who know about cars are probably smiling as they read this. Those who know nothing about cars must wait until the meal is finished.

I relaxed back in the restaurant. Someone of sober being would have to be called to take us safely home. She paid the tab, we got in the car, she put the key in the ignition, and without missing a single beat, the motor was humming. The terror ride was back on the road. After some incredible near misses, we made it home. Bad luck? I refused to believe it. Coincidence at best.

Second, my roommate wanted to smoke some marijuana. At that time, I had never used drugs but had heard all kinds of horrifying stories about it. In fact, the one circulating around most at the time was that marijuana was being laced with rat poisoning.

My roommate did not know where to get the stuff. I volunteered to talk to a neighborhood friend who smoked the stuff all the time. I met her and asked if she could get some marijuana for a party my roommate was having. She agreed to talk to a friend who was a member of the Hell's Angels.

During his trip of delivering the "pot" he got busted by the police. It was a set up, they believed. I was already suspected of being a narc, anyway. It all made sense to them. I must have tipped the police off.

I was given this message: Be at the swimming pool next Wednesday night at 9:00. I would be picked up by other members of the Hell's Angels who would take me to a trial. If the other members believed my story, I would be set free. If not, I would be dumped into the Savannah River.

Third, the morning following the drug bust I was informed by police that I was suspect in the robbery of a local band's musical equipment. I fit the description. The band members, whom I had never met, believed I was the thief. These band members probably saw me many times guarding the swimming pool and believed I matched the identity of local witnesses.

Fourth, I was kicked out of military school. For some reason I could not stay awake in class. In military training school, a soldier got "stars" when doing something wrong. Maybe this was some type of crack on military generals, I don't know. But you could only receive a maximum of four stars. A fifth star (that is the maximum number of stars a general can receive), and you are kicked out. Every time a soldier is caught sleeping, a star is "awarded." Several stars can be "awarded" in a single day.

I must have set a record for star gathering. In one day I was made a general and sent packing out of school. I simply could not stay awake. Once kicked out of school, the military then decides what to do with you. They are in no hurry. While awaiting re-assignment, I was placed on lawn detail, mowing the grass of some pretty large yards.

Fifth, my roommate decided to have his drug party anyway. But instead of getting marijuana, he got downers. To this day I have no idea what type of downers.

The drug party took place on a weeknight. But before revealing the outcome, it must be said that both of us were top secret military personnel. The fact that I had been kicked out of school did not negate my top secret clearance or absolve me of the top secret information I knew.

I don't remember how many of us were at the drug party. I had never done any sort of illicit drugs before. But on this night, with a room full of people on drugs, I decided to join in, not really knowing the effects of what I was ingesting.

Both of us slept for two days straight — the most noticeable effect, at least for me, of taking downers.

The military brass were looking for us — two top secret personnel were either missing, kidnapped, or (the dreaded) Away Without Leave (AWOL). We were AWOL.

Sixth, I lost every security clearance known to man. I turned myself in to the military. Immediately I was hauled into a room of wall-to-wall brass. I was seated in the middle. Life had crumbled.

There I sat, thinking of all that had happened in less than a week: kicked out of school, loss of all security clearances, placed on lawn-cutting detail, caught living off-base, caught using illegal drugs, AWOL, the Hell's Angels were after me, the police suspected me for the theft of a band's musical equipment. Now I'm seated in a room where surely one of the exit doors must have led to a firing squad.

Get a government job, I was told. Security, retirement — well, maybe retirement.

I can't really explain it. I cracked.

How I longed to be in a car with a drunken mother going down the wrong side of a four-lane highway.

She was a witch. No question about it. It started just as she said. The bad luck would be gradual, continually getting worse over the period of two weeks. How much worse could it get?

The military inquisition was short. I admitted to living off-base. I admitted to drug use. I admitted to being AWOL. They confronted me about getting kicked out of military school. They told me my security clearances were revoked.

"What has happened to you?" the top brass wanted to know.

Should I really tell them? I thought. It was all pretty obvious to me who was *really* at fault. But first I demanded utter secrecy.

I was assured — absolutely assured — that nothing I said would ever leave the confines of the room's four inner walls.

"A witch did it to me."

Seventh, I was put under psychiatric care.

Eighth, I was issued an "Article 15." That's something just shy of a court-martial. The punishment and fines associated with an "Article 15" make lawn detail seem like a trip to the ice cream parlor.

If possible, I would have gladly told the witch she was a witch. But I was confined to the military base. I had no way of breaking this witch's spell.

Ninth, a call from headquarters.

"Private Mawyer?"

"Yes, sir?

"Report to headquarters, your parents are here to see you."

My parents? In Augusta, Georgia? No way. What would they be doing here?

I got the sick, queasy feeling that my confidential — "never to be disclosed outside these four walls" — meeting was somehow violated.

Not surprisingly, my parents told me they got a call from the base commander telling them I was a drug addict suffering from hallucinations.

Now I'm a drug addict? Having hallucinations?

I tell my parents the same story I told the military brass, everything. At the time, I thought it was a pretty sound idea. After all, they were my parents. Surely they would believe that what appears to be hallucinations from drugs is really the doings of a witch.

Tenth, my parents affirm that I'm crazy. Now, if you think God really has His work cut out before Him, this *is not* the incident I referred to earlier as landing me in a military mental ward. That's a completely different story.

I explained to my parents that Augusta, Georgia, is really a strange town. Bizarre things happen here. I tell them about other incidents. With every breath, my words dig a deeper hole.

Not even a week has passed and I end up in a drunk driving adventure, the Hells Angels are closing in on my heels, the police still view me as a suspect for a crime I did not commit, I take drugs for the first time in my life, I am charged with being AWOL, I'm under psychiatric care, I'm kicked out of school, I'm issued an Article 15, I'm broke from the fines I have to pay, I'm labeled a drug addict who is suffering severe mental hallucinations, I learn that my superiors think keeping a secret means "within a 400 mile radius" — and they have the audacity to revoke my security clearance!

Now my parents arrive from Maryland and think I'm completely nuts.

I knew what I had to do, but the request to my parents was understandably difficult. "You've got to take me to see the daughter of this great white witch."

"There are no such things as witches," they said.

Yea, I thought, *well you better be careful who you tell that one to.*

They took me back to the apartment complex anyway. There I found her. Fortunately, she hadn't moved to Salem.

I still remember struggling to mouth the words, which seemed so insulting to me, "You are a witch."

"Had some bad luck, did you?"

"Yes," was my only reply.

"Now that you admit I'm a witch, I'll undo the bad luck."

Right, I thought. Just getting it to stop was enough for me.

What happened over the next few days was equally, if not more, astounding.

Five items were of immediate concern to me, in this order: (1) Getting the Hell's Angles off my back. (2) Getting the police off my back. (3) Getting my parents to believe I wasn't on drugs, suffering from hallucinations, or otherwise crazy. (4) Getting my security clearances back. (5) Getting back in school (never thought I'd hear myself say that one).

But I told none of these things to the witch. And, as far as I know to this day, she had no way of knowing anything that had happened over the course of that week.

The first two problems were solved the following day. The arrested Hell's Angel learned who the real narc was. The meeting and trial was called off.

The police made an arrest in the case of the stolen band's equipment.

Two down, three to go.

That night, my parents decided to camp out at a large military campground. It was late at night and a campfire was burning. Hardly another soul was camping. But I warned my parents this town was strange, so what happened next did not surprise me.

A young boy, about 10 years old, came running by the camp fire screaming, "Help, they're going to kill me."

We leaped up and asked, "Who's going to kill you?"

"My mother and sisters."

"Why?"

"Because I escaped from my cage."

Sure enough, right behind the small child was a knife-wielding mother and several daughters.

Not being experts in such drama, we handled this incident the best we could, though rather poorly.

"What are you doing?"

"We're going to catch him and put him back in his cage," the mother replied.

Minus the killing part, it was exactly what the boy said. The mother *was* holding a rather large butcher knife, however.

We told the boy to run off and demanded the girls stay, putting our bodies between them and the scurrying boy. We then told the girls to go back to where they came from. They turned around and walked away.

No, I do not know what happened to the boy. Never will, I suppose. My parents were not going to get any further involved.

But I asked my parents after they left, "Still think I'm crazy? How would it sound if *you* told this story to someone else?"

Case closed with my parents.

Three down, two to go.

The next day I was called into headquarters again. My commander told me that my security clearance was being reinstated.

"Why?" I asked.

"Someone signed a form vouching for you."

"What does the form say?"

"It says he or she will be personally responsible if you ever disclose any confidential or secret information."

"Who signed it?"

"I can't tell you."

I asked my parents. They did not sign it. The witch couldn't have, she knew nothing about it. To this day, I have no idea who signed the form.

"You are being re-admitted to school. You are to start as soon as your leave with your parents ends."

I asked no questions why, figured it had something to do with whoever signed the form.

Furthermore, I was ordered to stop receiving psychiatric care.

Suddenly, everything was as it had been. The only remaining sign that anything happened at all was the Article 15, which was a permanent part of my military record.

Everything happened just as the witch said it would. All the bad luck was undone. This is not an attempt to heap honor, praise, or worthiness on the witch. Far from it. It's just a statement of fact.

But my eyes were clearly open to mysterious, strange, and unseen powers.

9

The Bad Trip

I graduated from military school and was stationed in Darmstadt, Germany. Drugs were plentiful.

After several weeks it became clear to me that barracks life was broken down into three social camps: those who abused drugs, those who abused alcohol, and those who were homosexual.

I chose drugs.

Marijuana was scarce in Germany, but hashish abounded. Hashish is a narcotic obtained from the hemp plant, the same plant which produces marijuana.

Hashish was everywhere. Coming into the barracks in large blocks, hashish was later cut down into smaller chunks for resale. To obtain hash, one simply needed to go on a door-to-door, barracks-to-barracks hunt.

For most of us, virtually our entire paycheck went to purchasing this drug. We'd sit in the barracks, smoke hash, socialize, and listen to rock music.

Every once in a while, the military command would hold a "raid" on the barracks to root the stuff out. But warning of the impending raid was always posted on the barracks' outer doors. Drugs were in such wide use in 1972 that the military commanders really didn't want to launch a real raid.

To test my theory, I "hid" what appeared to be drugs in aluminum foil inside my locker. When the inspection team found the suspicious package, they simply put it back in the locker. They never opened it.

During the rare periods when hashish was not available, we popped acid pills — hallucinogens, which cause illusions.

Social life became nothing more than doing drugs.

Whether doing drugs was proper or not was never really questioned — American youth were in revolt. Besides, the military gave no appearance of caring one way or the other.

After several months of smoking and ingesting illegal substances, I concluded drugs were fine. I saw no harmful effects. I could still think, work, and be responsible in my duties. Older adults had their own drug, it was called alcohol. How self-righteous of them to ban our drugs.

During this time, I started reading a book by

James Michener called, *The Source*. The story began with the first steps of mankind and his relationship to God. God, in Michener's story of early man, played an active role in every part of community life. God was an interceder to these primitive human beings. God wasn't someone who just sat in the heavens watching mankind. Neither was God just a part of their lives. God *was* their life.

I read with great intensity. No one had ever presented God to me as anything more than a street conductor — these souls go to heaven, these souls go to hell.

I wanted what these primitive people had: a God that cared, listened, helped, directed, and loved.

Did such a God really exist? I was fascinated with the thought of working alongside God for a purpose.

I couldn't help but remember the tremendous powers that witch had over my life — for bad.

Does this mean God uses His tremendous powers over man's life — for good?

I read more of Michener's book. With every flipping page, God seemed more real, more caring, more involved.

I wanted this God, I just didn't know whether He really existed or not.

I went to the base library and checked out a Bible. I had three weeks to read it and then return it. I had no money to buy a Bible . . . all my money was hocked for drugs.

I started with the New Testament. The books

seemed shorter and easier to read. Besides, I was reading the life of God's son, Jesus. Certainly if God was involved with day-to-day mankind, He'd be involved with His own Son.

I read about miracles and healings. I read about God's plan for man. I read about God's love and forgiveness.

I breezed through the New Testament and read it again and again because the Bible was due back soon.

What fascinated me most was God's power, His realness, His personal relationship with each and every human being.

This was starkly different than anything I had ever heard about God, that He was somewhere, but nobody really knew where. In fact, some academician had recently declared God dead.

God did leave behind the Ten Commandments, but if we violated them we would go to hell. There was only one way out of these eternal flames and that was to accept Jesus Christ as your Saviour. But once you did, you had to follow these Ten Commandments. *What a bore,* I thought.

To me, that's all it meant to be a Christian. Accept forgiveness and then follow the Ten Commandments.

After reading the New Testament and Michener's, *The Source,* I determined that God was different, that He was more, that He was still alive. In fact, I refused to believe anything I had previously heard about God. I would simply discover God on my own.

First, I accepted this Jesus Christ as my Lord and

Saviour. This time I meant it. I knew exactly what I was doing.

Then I felt I needed to know whether drugs were wrong. They brought pleasure to me and were a big part of my life. I seriously questioned whether God forbade their use.

So I prayed, "God if drugs are wrong, show me."

The answer was but hours away.

That night about a half-dozen of my buddies and I went to a rock concert. No hashish was available, only LSD, a hallucinogen. LSD comes in the form of a pill, smaller than a sharpened pencil lead. Some druggies took as many as 60 of these pills at once. I pleaded to only take half of a pill. I rarely used hallucinogens, only when absolutely nothing else was available. But the supplier balked at cutting one of these pills in half. So for one dollar I bought a single hit of LSD.

The affect of the pill took about half an hour. Unlike any hallucinogen I had taken before, this one seemed extraordinarily powerful. Typically, hallucinogens brought only occasional illusions. Not this one.

Suddenly, everybody around me seemed artificial. Nobody was real. I could touch them; I could hear them; but I wasn't a part of their world any longer. I was incredibly withdrawn. There was me . . . and then there was everybody outside me. They had a strange yellowish color to them. They were having fun, but I wasn't a part of that life any longer.

My friends noticed my distancing. Perhaps they could see it in my eyes, my actions, or my words. They started talking to me — it's the first step in helping someone get out of a bad trip. But it didn't work. Things got worse.

Beyond my immediate vision, the whole auditorium was changing. It became a circus. It became a Roman arena with bombs blasting everywhere. It became a giant hand waving at me. It became a restaurant with everybody staring and pointing their fingers at me.

I had to get out. The whole room was shrinking and closing in on me. Nothing was real anymore — not the auditorium, not the seats, not my friends. I couldn't stop it.

Suddenly I went into convulsions. My *God,* I thought, *I'm going to die.* But I stopped the convulsions. I don't know how, I just stopped them because I was determined not to die.

Then something more strange took place. I heard the sound of something being sucked into me . . . and then the hallucinations suddenly stopped.

But now I was being told things. The words weren't audible. They were like talking silently to yourself. You know what's being said, but the words belonged to somebody else.

"You're going to die. . . . This crowd is going to crush you to death. . . ."

I had to get out. I walked out of the arena but stopped when it came time to cross the street to get to the parked car.

"You're going to get run over," I heard. "You're hallucinating . . . you'll never see the car that's going to hit you."

I couldn't move. The voice was right. How could

I trust my eyes crossing the street when I had just watched an entire auditorium turn into a giant hand?

I waited for others to cross the street with me.

"Are these people real? Or are you just seeing them?"

I ran across the street.

My party arrived shortly afterwards. They tried to talk me out of my bad trip, they stuck with me after I got back. But nothing worked. The voice would not be stopped.

It's impossible to describe what I felt. It was like losing your soul, like losing that part of you that says, "I'm me." I could not control my thoughts. I couldn't concentrate on anything anyone was saying. If, at the rock concert, I felt everyone was outside my world, I now felt I was outside my own body.

Maybe I should get away from these people, I thought. They were talking me to death and I didn't understand anything they were saying. I wanted to go back to my room.

It was dead winter in Germany. It was late and it was freezing outside. I got into my room and my entire body was shivering to the bone. I just wanted to get warm, lay down, and sleep this nonsense off.

I went to the radiator heater. It was ice cold. I tried turning it up, but it was already turned up full blast. *Impossible,* I thought. I felt it again. Ice cold.

The temperature in the room continued to drop. *This has never happened before,* I thought.

I kept my clothes on and quickly got under the covers. "Lord, don't let me die," I prayed.

"But you will die," a voice returned. "You've sinned against God. You told Him to show you if drugs were wrong and now He's showing you."

I reached up for my borrowed Bible. "Just words," the voice said. "Paper and ink. That Bible doesn't mean a thing if you're not going to follow it. Those words have to be *in you,* not in that Book you're holding."

The voice was right, I thought. Just paper and ink. I asked God to show me what's wrong with drugs and He's going to show me by killing me.

"Okay God. Let me die. I give up. I was wrong."

I stopped struggling against the tremendous force that waged its war against me. I relaxed, knowing death awaited me. I never closed my eyes though. I didn't have the courage.

I spiraled. Suddenly, everything in the room turned red. I saw objects beginning to float. I heard screaming . . . and this time the sounds *were* audible. Then I heard musical horns accompanying the screams. But the horns were off kilter — horrible, horrible sounds, like the horns were trying to scream, too.

My God, I'm going to hell, I thought.

I started to fight back. My will to live rekindled.

The sounds stopped. The objects in the room came back to rest. Everything returned to its original color.

I can't die, not yet.

I never slept a wink. The voice talked, talked, and talked. Morning came. I couldn't eat. It didn't want me to. It didn't want me to sleep. It didn't want me to talk to anybody. It had almost complete control.

I was his, whoever he was.

I tried watching television, anything to divert my attention. But I literally could not see the picture on the screen. The frames were out of sync with my eyes.

I couldn't take it anymore. I needed help, any kind of help. I turned myself in to the base medical center. I was immediately shipped to an Army hospital in Frankfurt.

I sat through admissions. Nurses, doctors, administrators — everyone was extraordinarily rude. I didn't blame them really. I was there on a drug overdose, something very preventable.

Furthermore, I gave the appearance I wasn't cooperating with their questions. "What's the name of your parents?" they'd ask.

"I don't remember," I'd reply.

It was taking over. I could only remember recent events. Things in the past were . . . well . . . gone.

In a single night, I was passed off to several psychiatrists. The first three were callous, cold, even hateful.

They then turned me over to a fourth psychiatrist. He asked the same questions: background, events, history. He was pleasant, however. I asked him why he was being so nice while everyone else had been so cruel?

His answer startled me: "You're demon possessed," he said. "They feel the presence of the demon in you, but don't believe in demons. They're responding angrily to the demonic spirit that's taken over your body. It's so strong, I can feel it."

Demon possessed? The suction feeling I felt right after the convulsions took place, the voice that won't go away, the reason why I feel like I lost my soul, the *it* I've been warring with . . . could it be a demon?

"The other doctors don't believe in demon possession?" I struggled to ask.

"No," he said.

"You do?"

"Yes. Your whole body has a demonic aura."

What the heck is an aura, I thought.

The "possession" lasted for days. Real or not, it gave me a focal point on what was happening.

The terror of those several days aren't worth repeating in detail. It was a battle over my soul, this I believed. At times the fear, voice, "possession" was so intense I had to be segregated from others.

I just kept praying for God to deliver me.

The battle was extraordinarily draining. I rarely slept. It wouldn't let me.

One afternoon, complete exhaustion finally consumed me and I fell asleep. I had a dream. It is as vivid today as it was those 21 years ago.

I was nothing but a soul in this dream. I had no body. I was flying frantically, looking for my body. I flew through doors and buildings. I flew up stairways and down stairways. I searched every living creature to see if it was me. Finally, I flew into a small room and there I was, just standing there, motionless. I leaped into my body.

At that point, I felt a tremendous crushing feeling on my body, like being squeezed in a vice. A loud pop rang out from my ears.

I was awakened immediately, from the force of this gripping feeling and the burst of its sound.

Something exploded out of my body. The voice was gone. The war over my body had ended. That feeling that *I'm me* had returned.

But *it* wasn't far away. I could see my body being poked at. Indentations were being pressed all over my legs, arms, chest, and stomach — like it was trying to get back in.

But I didn't worry. If the Lord allowed me to survive these days and kick it out, certainly the Lord and I could keep it out.

I went to the psychiatrists and told them I was healed.

"It is gone!" I said.

"How did *it* leave?" they asked.

"Jesus delivered me."

"Where is this Jesus now?"

"He lives in me?"

"So, now Jesus is living in you?" they asked.

Somehow, I knew where this line of questioning was leading. But I didn't care. Christ delivered me and I was excited.

"Yes, Christ lives in me."

"Christ died 2,000 years ago."

"Yes, but He was resurrected."

"So, instead of a demon, you now have a 2,000-year-old dead man living in you?"

The looks in their eyes told me I'd be hanging around the mental ward for some time to come.

10

No Way Out

I was eventually transferred back to the states and placed in Walter Reed Medical Hospital — an army hospital treating United States presidents and, of course, mentally insane soldiers.

I wasn't alone. Nary a bed in the ward was ever empty. Most patients were there for the same reason: drug abuse causing mental delusions.

Soldiers were placed in close quarters, a bed being your only private space. Everything else was shared by a community of patients.

Psychiatrists lined you up — twice a day — to pop pills, drink medications, and take needles. More drugs were dispensed in that place than I saw in all of

Germany. If you weren't crazy before you went in, you probably would be by the time you got out—if you ever got out.

Since no one was "normal," you heard bizarre stories all day long. Some inmates were extremely violent and you had no way to protect yourself. The medication was intentionally designed to turn you into a walking zombie. After a while you could hardly think.

Everyday was virtually the same. Get up. Take some medicine. Talk to someone who thinks he's an alien — or worse. Go to group studies, listen to more bizarre tales and actions. Talk to your counselor or psychiatrist. Take some more medication. Then go back to bed and start the process over again the next day.

If you behaved yourself, you were allowed to work somewhere in the hospital, such as a clerk or filing. Some days you were allowed to go outside and play a sport. But this all depended on your progress and behavior.

Even the psychiatrist's questions were routine and redundant. "What does, 'A rolling stone gathers no moss,' mean to you?" he'd ask me.

"What's moss?" I'd ask.

Without a blink (or an answer) he'd make a note in his pad.

"What does, 'A person living in a glass house shouldn't throw stones,' mean to you?"

"I don't know. He'd break windows if he did?"

More scribbling.

"Are you still demon possessed?"

"No." Finally, something I could understand.

"Why aren't you demon possessed?" he'd ask.

"Jesus delivered me."

"How?"

"He came to live in my life."

"Where exactly is He living?"

"In me."

"How did He get in you?"

"By accepting His forgiveness."

"Does He talk to you?"

"Yes."

"You can hear Him?"

"Not audibly, but He does speak to me."

"The demon used to speak to you, too. Isn't that right?"

"Yes."

"The demon told you bad things?"

"Yes."

"What does Jesus tell you?"

"Lots of things: What not to do. What to do. How to please Him. How to treat others."

"How long will Jesus live in you?"

"Until I die."

"Don't you think you just replaced something bad with something you think is good?"

"Yes, but Jesus is real."

"Wasn't the demon real?"

"Yes, he was real too."

"Does the demon ever bother you anymore?"

"Well, Satan will always throw obstacles in my way."

"What kind of obstacles? Chairs? Tables?"

"No. I mean temptations to sin."

"Does Jesus control you?"

"I try to let Him."

"He wants to take over your body?"

"Well, He wants me to become Christ-like."

"So Jesus wants you to become like Him?"

"Yes."

"How much will you let Him control?"

"All of me, I hope."

"We'll talk tomorrow."

At the time, I desperately wanted out of the hospital. I felt I was normal. Accepting Jesus in my life may not be what these doctors personally wanted, but they couldn't possibly think everyone who accepts Jesus is crazy.

I wanted to convince them that I was normal. But the more I talked, the more they appeared to think I was insane. I didn't know what they were looking for. But it began to worry me because they asked the same questions, over and over again. I wasn't about to change my story, but I wasn't sure I'd ever get out unless I did.

They made it perfectly clear to me that I was still mentally deluded. They felt I had just replaced one possession with another type of possession: I exchanged an evil spirit for a good spirit. They couldn't understand how I could believe a dead man was living in me or why I would let this dead man control my body. They believed I just picked the most benevolent dead person I knew to replace the evil one that had been in control. It could have been any dead person, as far as they were concerned, as long as I felt he was better than the evil one that had left me.

The bottom line to these psychiatrists was that I was no longer in control of my body, my actions, or my future. Such loss of personal control, or the specter of being guided by unseen spirits or the voices of dead people, meant I could present a danger to myself or to others.

In their logic, they had to be convinced that this dead person, whom I called Jesus, was not going to cause harm.

Life in the mental ward got worse. The mind-bending drugs were beginning to take their toll. My thought process was coming to a halt. I wanted to live, but I didn't know what I wanted to live for. All I wanted to do was sleep. I had never heard of the drug I was taking, Thorazine, but I was up to 600 milligrams a day — an astoundingly high dosage I would later find out. I would also find out later that Thorazine is best known for turning its users into zombies.

Medically, Thorazine is supposed to help the mentally disturbed by turning off the thinking process. It *did* turn off the thinking process. But I'd hardly say it was helping me.

Since I had no idea what I was taking, or the effects of the drug, I thought I was truly losing my mind — and indeed I was, because that's what the doctors wanted.

If the drug worked, I'd stop thinking about this dead man who wanted to control my body, soul, and spirit.

But Thorazine doesn't just stop you from thinking about dead people — it just plain stops you from thinking. I had no ambition. No care. No desires. No goals. I couldn't make sense of anything. I was just living, day to day, for no apparent reason I could think of.

I still read the Bible, but I could hardly see the words anymore. Another side effect of Thorazine is that it blurs vision. The medical staff, however, told me none of the drug's side effects. I just thought I was losing my sight.

I became tremendously depressed, another of the drug's side effects. But again, I didn't know why.

The drug that brought me into the hospital was LSD. The drug that threatened to keep me there was Thorazine.

I was dying from boredom and the will to do nothing. I couldn't understand why, when I was first admitted, the staff had such a hard time getting patients to make up their beds, socialize, stay awake, or get involved in activities. Such things seemed so simple.

But now I was one of them.

It wasn't until the army psychiatrists agreed that Christ presented no danger to myself or others that I was finally allowed to leave. But even though I left, they forever tagged me as being 50 percent mentally disabled because I believed Christ should be allowed to rule my life.

11

The Dream

When the army sent me packing, my future looked bleak — no college education, barely graduated from high school, kicked out of the armed services, discharged from a mental ward, a drug abuser, and classified as 50 percent mentally disabled by the United States Army.

Obviously, I had to take jobs that didn't ask a lot of probing questions — a forklift operator, a janitor, a seller of pots and pans, a courier, a roofer, a construction worker.

For the most part, I looked at these jobs as entry level positions which would eventually lead somewhere. But these jobs either led to being fired, laid off, or physical problems.

Most often I gravitated toward physical labor jobs, for obvious reasons — no questions, no résumés, no experience needed. But I was hardly cut out for physical labor. I stood less than 5 feet 8 inches and weighed about 135 pounds.

I was dwarfed by men almost twice my weight, four inches taller in height, and who had arms the size of my neck. But I was expected to keep up with them, carry what they carried, and be just another brute.

I hated going to work. I couldn't understand why God put me in jobs I wasn't physically capable of performing and hated doing at the same time. It made no sense.

I told my church leaders my frustration. They asked me what I liked doing and I said writing. But they told me a writer needs something to write about and I really had nothing to say. They suggested I go to college and take up a career in something more promising.

I chose civil engineering. I really can't explain why. I hated math. I had no math background, skipping out on chemistry, physics, geometry, and algebra in high school. I had never even heard of logarithm or calculus.

But I was undeterred. Civil engineering sounded important, it paid well, and there was a demand for engineers.

The first semester began in January and was nothing but remedial courses. I passed the remedial courses and began the fall in a serious attempt at a civil engineering career.

Things were looking great, until I took logarithm. I simply could not remember the mathematical formulas. I understood how to do the equations, but come test time, the formulas were long forgotten.

I was flunking the course. I dropped the class, and therefore dropped out of civil engineering.

Then I remembered that third-grade teacher who told me to go to college to be a journalist. I was but eight years old at the time, but she believed I could write.

I believed I could write. I loved writing. I tried everybody else's advice and was getting nowhere in life. Everyone, but this third-grade teacher, told me all the reasons I could never be a writer. No one I talked to believed God gave me this writing ability so I could be a writer — including the church pastor and elders.

Writing was viewed as non-work, a dream, an egotistical fantasy, an irresponsible venture, something only rich people have the luxury to do.

But this time I didn't listen to others. I listened to what I wanted to do, what I loved, what I felt I was best at. I decided to follow the emotions and talents God put within me, in hopes that it was God's will. I enrolled in journalism.

Little did I know that with this decision, God was fashioning a tremendous turning point in my life.

After the first semester, I aced my courses. After my second semester, I aced my courses. One year in college and I had a 4.0 grade-point average.

Summer came and my wife became pregnant with our first child. She worked for the federal government and largely supported our family. I had no choice but to finish the semester and get a job, in hopes of finishing college on a part-time schedule.

I went back to construction, building residential homes. But construction life had changed. Instead of building homes stick by stick, they were being pre-fabricated — large sections of walls already built and ready to be carted and erected through brute strength.

These walls weighed as much as 400 pounds. I still only weighed 135 pounds. After a month, I suffered a serious back injury.

My entire right side became numb. My back was filled with pain. Like most back injuries, the actual damage was impossible to locate. The only treatment was lying in bed.

I was terror-stricken. How would I support my family? One year in college does not make for a white-collar career — especially with my background. All blue-collar jobs required some type of physical labor, which I could no longer do. And this came at a time when a baby was on the way.

I was crushed, confused, and angry. In just a few months my family would be without any money what-soever. I couldn't even take a job sitting down, my back hurt so much. I saw nothing good that could come out of this. As far as I knew, my back might never get better. To make matters worse, I had nothing but time to contemplate the coming catastrophe.

I tried with all my mind to trust in God. But my mind left me with no options or solutions. I saw no hope, not even the flickering of a faint light.

To be without a job is to feel rejected, useless, an outcast, and at fault. You fear losing your home and car.

You have no idea how you'll buy food or pay the heating bill. You envision being thrown out on the streets, your family starving, your relatives blaming you.

You are embarrassed to meet people. You feel like a failure in life. You have to live with the people you're hurting everyday, with no possibility of escape. Your fears imprison your emotions, thoughts, and responses.

Nothing makes you feel more like a wasted member of society than to be without the means to support your family.

I knew not what to do or where to go.

If God would have spared me the back injury, I thought, *I could at least look for a job and finish college eventually.* But with the back injury, all was lost.

Never in my life had I felt so hopeless, so frustrated, so helpless.

Just when I thought I discovered what God wanted me to do, I was at life's lowest ebb. None of the troubles or difficulties I faced before were even close to this — before I was only hurting myself, not my wife and child-to-be.

I complained to God. Would anything good in life ever come to me? Or will my life be just one tragedy after another?

Then God reminded me of the Israelites in the wilderness. They too grumbled, bemoaned, whimpered, and complained. The result? They died in the wilderness.

I was indeed in a wilderness — a wilderness of want and confusion. If God was going to compare my grumblings with those of the Israelites in the wilderness, I decided to re-read the biblical story to find out what God truly expected of these people.

The answer was plainly clear — trust, faith, and hope. God did not make life easy for the fleeing Israelites. They hungered and thirsted. They fought enemies. They needed mighty miracles to survive — the splitting of the Red Sea, water from a rock, strange manna growing mysteriously in the mornings, quail dropping miraculously from the sky in the evenings.

But what really struck me was that most of these miracles never happened until the last minute — when all seemed lost and hopeless, when days of slavery seemed far better than the Promised-Land-to-be, when impending death seemed so near.

God tested and re-tested the faith of the Israelites. Forget an eleventh hour God. God often waited until 11:59.

It wasn't that God couldn't have chosen to come through earlier, He simply didn't want to. Why? Because faith is a believer's most precious possession in the sight of God, more precious than silver or gold.

Before entering the Promised Land, these Israelites would learn faith, or die trying. Virtually all died.

The lesson was clear. Grumbling against God during times of turmoil could keep you out of the Promised Land. Faith, in spite of impending doom and gloom, will get you into the Promised Land, flowing with milk and honey.

The first tests, then, in achieving the good works God has called you to do are tests of faith. It makes sense. How could God ever expect you to complete the good works He has called you to do if you don't have complete faith?

Remember, the Promised Land didn't look too promising at first. There were physical giants in the land. Enemies were there too. Faith was needed there as well. The walls of Jericho still had to be demolished.

I immediately stopped grumbling.

Within a couple of weeks, a church friend came to my home and told me about some business equipment he had just sold to a religious news service. He didn't know much about it, but knew I was interested in writing and just wanted to pass the information along.

The news service was located in Washington, DC. I lived in Laurel, Maryland, about 30 minutes away.

An open door? I didn't know. I had every reason not to go — no experience, no diploma. And let's not forget, Washington, DC is full of aspiring journalists with degrees, experience, and recommendations to boot.

On the whim that this could be God, I went.

I reached the offices in a downtown building and learned that the news service was owned by an editor of the former *Washington Star.* I asked if I could write a news story.

The request was met with predictable questions. What experience do you have? Where did you graduate? How long have you been writing?

Of course, I had to give a negative answer to all these questions.

"I'm sorry," I was told.

I took another stab. "Could I just write a news story for you to look at? If you don't like it, I'll go away."

"I'm sorry, but no," came the response.

I was quite discouraged, but determined not to grumble or complain.

I went home and decided to write something anyway. I had nothing but time on my hand. What could I lose?

I didn't know what kind of religious news service the agency specialized in, but I had read something about a school prayer bill before the United States Congress.

I dug into library books to learn as much as I could about the school prayer issue. I then started calling congressional offices and activist groups.

When I finished my research I wrote a news story and took it to the religious news service.

They weren't exactly happy to see me again.

But they agreed to read the story — probably in hopes of telling me how bad it was so I'd go away and bother someone else.

The managing editor read it and gave it to the production editor, who read it and took it to the owner.

The owner was William (Bill) Willoughby, one of the giants in the religious news industry.

He read it in my presence, looked up and asked, "Where did you learn to write like this?"

I wasn't sure if he meant *good* like this or *horrible* like this.

"Nowhere. I just used the inverted pyramid." I wanted to sound like I at least knew something about journalism.

"I've met few people who have put this much effort in a news story before. It's good. What do you want, a job?"

"Yes."

"Okay, I'll pay you $50 a story. You can write three stories a week."

He then introduced me to everyone else and showed me my office. An office? I never had an office before. I tried not to show my shock, but there was a desk, chair, telephone, and a typewriter, too.

I'd have to wear a business suit to work. I was truly embarrassed to wear business suits — I felt like an impostor masquerading as a businessman every time I put one on. The only business suit I saw growing up was on my father at a funeral.

But best of all — even without a degree, without any experience, without any background I'd care to repeat — I would write for a living.

I was so excited I had to tell someone. I called my pastor. He wasn't pleased. In fact, he was extremely sarcastic, "Wow, $150 a week, huh? You can buy a lot with that."

He didn't understand. It was the dream, not the money. It was what I loved. It was a miracle from God. It was the impossible made possible.

It was what everybody told me I'd never be able to do . . . except for a third-grade teacher, whose name I have long forgotten.

12

An Equal Opportunity God

The re-telling of my life's early years — though engaging — was meant as an example. You can start now on your chosen course.

It doesn't matter what your background, experience, or education is, who's against you, how impossible the goal, or how big the mess — God is waiting for you to begin.

Start by choosing what you like most and believe you would be best at doing. I call this your dominant talent. It's something God will wrap many of your other talents around.

Don't quit your job, leave the country, bolt for Hollywood, or act irrational in any way. Let God put the pieces of the puzzle together.

Begin simply. Find a way, however small, to develop your dominant talent. Be faithful and pray that God opens all the doors to move you along.

Remember, "He who is faithful in a very little thing is faithful also in much; and he who is unrighteous in a very little thing is unrighteous in much" (Luke 16:10).

Don't expect God to open any doors if you're going to bury your talent. You begin by making small investments — in time, practice, and development.

We have already examined the parable of the talents in Matthew 25, and the worthless slave who buried his talent in the ground.

But there is another parable told in Luke 19, similar to the parable of the talents, but different, nevertheless. It's the parable of the minas. In this case, the master gave each slave the same number of minas, one each.

Like the parable of the talents, the slaves were told to go out and do business until the master returned.

One slave took his mina and turned it into 10 minas more. He was placed in charge of 10 cities. Another took his mina and turned it into five minas more. He was placed in charge of five cities. Another took his mina and put it away in a handkerchief. His mina was taken away from him and given to the slave who already had 10.

The parable concludes: "I tell you, that to everyone who has shall more be given, but from the one who does not have, even what he does have shall be taken away" (Luke 19: 26).

There has been much scholarly discussion about the similarities of the parable of the talents and minas. Some scholars say the parables are one and the same, simply told differently. But close examination of the two parables shows many distinct differences. There were differing numbers of slaves, differing amounts of money handed out by the nobleman, differing returns on investments, differing rewards, differing punishments, and more.

I believe the two parables are disparate and offer separate meanings.

It is not the purpose of this examination to discuss all the differing meanings and aspects of the two parables. The only focus I want to draw attention to is the differing amounts of money each slave was given to invest. In the parable of the talents, the amounts given to each slave were five, two, and one. In the parable of the minas, each slave was given the same amount of money, one mina each.

I believe the mina, in this parable, represents opportunity. Though each of us may have a differing number of talents, God gives all of us equal opportunity for success in God's unique calling.

No one can claim God gave more opportunity to one Christian than another. We may argue that God has given more talents to one Christian than to another, but not more opportunity to succeed with those talents.

Furthermore, this parable ends by saying those

who have shall be given more, and those who do not have shall lose what they do have.

In other words, those who take advantage of the opportunity presented them by God shall be given more opportunities in this life. When the Master comes, these good slaves shall be rewarded by being given authority relative to the number of opportunities taken. Those who squander opportunity in this life, however, will not be given any more opportunity. These worthless slaves shall be given authority over nothing when the Master returns.

Notice the word *worthless* in both parables regarding the slave who buried his talent and put away his mina.

Those of us who fail to use our talents for God or fail to take advantage of God-given opportunity are worthless. To be worthless is to be useless. How can God possibly use us if we bury our talents and put away God-given opportunity?

To be Christian, and useful to God, is not simply to be a vessel of gold and silver. Read this Scripture carefully:

> Now in a large house there are not only gold and silver vessels, but also vessels of wood and of earthenware, and some to honor and some to dishonor.
>
> Therefore, if a man cleanses himself from these things, he will be a vessel for honor, sanctified, *useful* to the Master, prepared for every good work (2 Tim. 2:20-21).

The point of cleansing and being a golden vessel is not for aesthetic beauty, but to be "useful to the Master, prepared for every good work." Those Christians whose only concentration is ridding themselves of sin and looking pretty are simply placed on a shelf. These will never "complete the course" as Paul did.

Many tarnished vessels are used mightily by God and many glowing ones remain sitting idly on the shelf — filled with jealousy and bewilderment as they look on.

God will use those who are available to Him — even if the vessel is far from golden or perfect. Just look at your own household as an example. How many times have you used the back end of a screwdriver because you didn't have a hammer, or used a butcher knife because you couldn't find a pair of scissors, or used a chair because you didn't have a step stool? You use what is available. So does God.

To be used by God is to be willing to invest your talents and take advantage of opportunity.

You start by taking advantage of the one opportunity you do have. This first opportunity is pretty simple. Look at your list of likes and dislikes. Find your dominant talent, that is, what you like best and what you believe you are best at doing. Begin using it, no matter how small the opportunity — because he who is faithful in a very little thing is also faithful in much.

There is another key thought in both parables: to be placed in charge when the Master returns. God is looking for Christians who will rule with Him in His eternal kingdom. During this life, God will find out who those ruling Christians are and decide how much authority will be given them.

Talent and opportunity — without them, authority is denied.

Take your own life as an example. Would you place someone in charge of your personal affairs if that person refuses to use any of his talents or fails to strike when opportunity arises? Of course not. Neither will God.

13

Where the Wind Blows

Once you make a decision to walk in the footsteps of God, you're on a path of unknown charter. You will not know where God is taking you.

I advise strongly against examining your likes and dislikes, and then making a concrete decision about where it is you will go or what it is you will be doing. The Bible is quite clear: you don't know.

"The wind blows where it wishes and you hear the sound of it, but do not know where it comes from and where it is going; so is *everyone* who is born of the Spirit" (John 3:8).

You are the wind, you do not know where you came from and where you are going in God.

At times, this becomes very frustrating — especially when all society, our family, and God expect us to take charge of our lives, to lead, direct, and have a plan. If we don't know where we are going, how can we possibly make short-term or long-term decisions about our lives? Obviously, a proper balance needs to be struck.

To strike that proper balance, you must understand that although God has not given you knowledge of the ultimate destination, He has at least given you a small glimpse of the road in front of you to follow.

That small glimpse always requires using your best talents for the kingdom of God and being responsible for the little that you do have. As long as you move your feet, God can redirect you if you walk off the chosen course. If you're standing still, however, you will go nowhere.

Let me relate a personal example.

When I was fired from Moral Majority as editor of the *Moral Majority Report,* I did not know where to go next. I kept my feet moving by applying for jobs that were somewhat related to my previous experience. The jobs I applied for, however, were a far stretch from what I wanted to do or where I thought God was taking my life. The only jobs available were for fundraising writers.

I was a journalist, not a fundraising writer. I thought my unique talent and calling of God was to educate Christians about current events that were important to them, their families, and to the Kingdom. I could not comprehend how helping an organization raise money for, say, the Panama Canal, figured into the game plan.

I took a freelance contract in Chantilly, Virginia —a three-hour drive from my home—with a fundraising agency, Richard A. Delgaudio and Associates. I accepted the six-month contract with mixed emotions. On the one hand, I was still writing, still involved in conservative politics, still providing for my family. On the other hand, I was no longer a journalist, no longer educating Christians about religious matters, no longer using many of my other skills — interviewing, layout design, editorial planning.

I had no idea how any of this fit into God's grand design for my life. At best, I thought, it was a temporary setback that allowed me to continue to use some of my skills.

I was driving to Chantilly one Monday morning when I questioned God about how this job fit into my life, why it was necessary to even suffer a temporary setback, and why I couldn't just move forward.

Then God told me to look at the road in front of me. I did. He asked how much of that road I could see. About a quarter of a mile. Then He asked whether I believed there was still a road beyond what I could see. I said yes. He asked if I needed to see the entire road on that three-hour trip to know that this road was taking me to my destination. Of course I didn't.

Even in our normal traveling, we only see a small stretch of road where we are headed. In God, you not only have no idea where you are ultimately going, but you don't even know what the road looks like on the other side. But, as in everyday life, you must follow at least what you can see.

I followed that road, having no idea what the outcome would be. Now I'm so thankful and grateful that God took me on it. While at Richard A. Delgaudio and Associates, I learned how to raise funds for worthy causes. Without that experience, God could never have taken me to the destination I am at today, founder of the Christian Action Network.

This illustration demonstrates balance in walking with God. God gave me talents and loves, the dominant talent being writing. I never gave up my responsibilities to lead, direct, or take charge of my life. And I never gave up my dominant talent. But I was flexible enough to allow the wind to blow me from one destination to another even though it made no sense at the time.

The Scripture I keep in my heart at all times in walking with God is this: "But the path of the righteous is like the light of dawn, that shines brighter and brighter until the full day" (Prov. 4:18).

The Scripture clearly makes note that the initial beginnings of our path are only dawn-lit, barely visible. But as we walk down that path, the sun shines brighter and brighter, and we see more and more clearly. Eventually it all makes sense at full day.

The key in all cases is being responsible for all that you can do to use your God-given talents and gifts for God. Then trust God. Even if your current status seems polars away from what would appear logical, trust God.

"Now faith is the assurance of things hoped for, the conviction of things not seen" (Heb. 11:1).

Whose life was a better example of this faith than that of the patriarch Joseph?

Joseph told this dream to his brothers: "For behold, we were binding sheaves in the field, and lo, my sheaf rose up and also stood erect; and behold, your sheaves gathered around and bowed down to my sheaf" (Gen. 37:7).

Then Joseph told this dream to his father. "Lo, I have had still another dream; and behold, the sun and the moon and eleven stars were bowing down to me."

His father rebuked him. His brothers wanted to kill him. God then used his brothers' anger to begin fulfilling the dream. Before I repeat what you already know about Joseph's life, think about what would be going through your mind if any one of these events — much less all of them — happened to you. Could you possibly see any good that could come from these events, would you lose faith, would you be enjoying the assurance and conviction of things not seen which faith brings?

Joseph was thrown into a pit, then sold to a caravan of Ishmaelites, then sold to a bodyguard, then thrown into prison. Then while in prison, to add insult to injury, the chief cupbearer — whom Joseph gave a favorable interpretation of a dream — forgot to mention Joseph to the Pharaoh to get him out of the dungeon.

God promised Joseph that his brothers (on one

occasion) and his father, mother, and brothers (on another occasion) would come bowing down to him. Now, 13 years later, he's rotting in prison with no timetable for release — forgotten even by the chief cupbearer. Without the hope of those dreams, Joseph could be a prisoner for the rest of his life. It took 27 years before that first dream was fulfilled!

How many of us would have given up, long ago, on God fulfilling that dream? All kinds of thoughts would be roaming through our heads. *God is punishing me for something I've done; God really didn't speak to me; I've failed God somewhere along the way; Satan is attacking me.*

Furthermore, you would have no support from family, relatives, or friends. Nothing in your life during those first 13 years would appear to be headed in the right direction. In fact, all evidence would indicate you're headed in a completely opposite path. Instead of your father, mother, and brothers bowing to you, you're in a dungeon, left for dead.

Because Joseph was given a dream, he was in a unique position not given most Christians. He had a vision where the wind would eventually blow him. I know of no Christian who's enjoyed such a vision.

But this point is extremely important: The dreams Joseph had were not his calling in life, they were the result of *fulfilling* his calling in life. God did not create Joseph so that his family would bow to him. His calling was much greater than that. His family bowed to him because of his faithfulness in doing the little things God did give him.

God never put Joseph in a position where he could not develop his talent and skills for taking charge. This is critical, because one day God would put Joseph in charge of an entire nation of people. The very lives of the Egyptians, and those of bordering countries, depended on the proper use of Joseph's skills and talents.

When Joseph was sold to the bodyguard, the captain "made him overseer in his house, and over all that he owned.... So he left *everything he owned* in his charge; and with him there he did not concern himself with anything except the food which he ate" (Gen. 39:5-6).

When Joseph was later thrown into prison by this bodyguard, the chief jailer "committed to Joseph's charge all the prisoners who were in the jail; so that whatever was done there, he was responsible for it. The chief jailer did not supervise anything under Joseph's charge because the Lord was with him; and whatever he did, the Lord made to prosper" (Gen. 39:22-23).

By the time Joseph came out of prison, he had experience in taking charge, being responsible for other people's lives, and supervising everything that needed to be done. So much so that the bodyguard simply concerned himself with what he ate, and the chief jailer concerned himself with nothing in the care of those prisoners. In both cases, Joseph was placed second in command only behind the bodyguard and chief jailer.

Keeping in mind Joseph's experience and faithfulness with the bodyguard and the chief jailer, read now Pharaoh's commissioning of Joseph:

"You shall be over my house, and according to your command all my people shall do homage; only in the throne I will be greater than you." And Pharaoh said to Joseph, "See I have set you over all the land of Egypt" (Gen. 41:40-41).

Clearly, Joseph was always on the path of his calling. All along, Joseph was responsible in the little things, developing his skills of leadership, wisdom, and authority. When the time came to put Joseph in charge of Egypt, he was not an inexperienced magistrate.

Another important point here is that God, not Satan, was responsible for Joseph being thrown into the pit by his brothers. Joseph even consoled his brothers with this assurance.

"And now do not be grieved or angry with yourselves, because you sold me here, for God sent me before you to preserve life" (Gen. 45:5).

"Now, therefore it was not you who sent me here, but God" (Gen. 45:8).

If I had a dream of having my family bow before me, and then I was thrown into a pit and sold as a slave to a traveling caravan by the very people who were supposed to bow to me, and I was then thrown in prison, I'd be blaming Satan. But instead of cursing Satan, I should be praising God.

Proper balance in walking with God has been outlined here. You do not know where God is taking you, but you are expected to continue to be faithful with the talents God has given you in what you do have.

I'm sure Joseph had no idea how being in a dungeon would lead to being in charge of a nation, but it did. If Joseph gave up, cowered in the corner of his cell, wept bitterly against God, raised his voice against Satan, refused to use his God-given gifts in whatever situation he was in, he might not have ever seen the dream come true.

"He who has found his life shall lose it, and he who has lost his life for My sake shall find it" (Matt. 10:39).

This Scripture is not referring to the afterlife alone.

To lose your life in Christ is to allow Him to use your whole being for His kingdom. Though this can be expanded upon, in reference to this discussion, it's to allow God to use your talents and emotions for His kingdom.

I have the talent to be a writer. But instead of being a novelist, I use my writing skills to defend God's truths. Fifteen years ago, when I landed my first job in journalism, I would never have thought it would lead to where I am today.

You and I don't own the talents and emotions given us — God owns them. We can steal these talents and emotions and use them for ourselves if we want to. If we want, we can ignore them or use them for our own purposes. We may even enjoy great success with them — as the world measures success. But in doing so, we will lose our life — that is, our life's calling, the "good work of the righteous *will be* granted" [emphasis added] (Prov. 10:24).

14

The Looking-Glass of Love

Whatever your talents are, God gave them to you for one primary purpose: to bless your fellow man. As you develop your skills, then find ways to apply your talents toward the benefit of mankind.

This is a basic tenet of every reputable business. Every product created is fashioned to meet the needs, desires, and demands of consumers. Those business-men who best meet those requests are typically awarded the most success.

I find this tenet no different in the kingdom of God. The gifts and callings of God were given you for the purpose of "good works." Those good works are for the benefit of others. The better your ability to meet the needs of mankind, the more success in God you will enjoy. Undergirding this success, then, are two motivations — the true desire to love and serve.

Some businessmen may enjoy great success without truly wanting to love and serve their customers. But our success is not measured in worldly standards of fame and fortune. Our success is measured by our ability to "finish the course."

The reason you're on the race course is to use your God-given talents for "good works." But every step of that track is paved with love. The runner, then, must be a servant.

"But now abide faith, hope, love, these three; but the greatest of these is love" (1 Cor. 13:13).

Love is more than action. Love is in the heart. There's a mystery here which I'll reveal in a moment. But first let's examine the problems of love defined as actions.

"And if I give all my possessions to feed the poor, and if I deliver my body to be burned, but do not have love, it profits me nothing" (1 Cor. 13:3).

This is quite a shocking statement. Can you imagine giving all your possessions to the poor and it *not* being done out of love? Better still, can you imagine giving your body to be burned and it *not* being done out of love?

Even the deepest of religious works can be performed without love.

"And if I have the gift of prophesy, and know all

mysteries and all knowledge; and if I have all faith, so as to remove mountains, but do not have love, I am nothing" (1 Cor. 13:2).

Elsewhere, Jesus says, "Many will say to Me on that day, 'Lord, Lord, did we not prophesy in Your name, and in Your name cast out demons, and in Your name perform many miracles?' And I will declare to them, 'I never knew you; DEPART FROM ME, YOU WHO PRACTICE LAWLESSNESS'" (Matt. 7:22-23, emphasis theirs).

Love results in actions. But the converse is not always true. Actions are not necessarily the result of love.

What the Scriptures tell us here, amazingly enough, is that great works and sacrifices can be fulfilled by a Christian and none of it be done out of love. Therefore, visual success — removing mountains, casting out demons, performing miracles, being burned — is *not* evidence, alone, of love.

The message, then, is a matter of focus. Let me explain. If we focus on worthy actions and deeds, we can probably perform such wonders but not necessarily perform them out of love. If we truly love from the heart, and let our heart guide our actions, then the performance is done strictly out of love. Therefore, God's love for fellow man must fill your heart.

If you focus on the love in your heart, you will know where to apply your talents. Love is directing you. If you think love is nothing but good actions, you will probably still use your talents successfully, but don't bring them up in the presence of the Lord in His coming, lest the Lord say, "Depart from me, you who practice lawlessness."

Love is the law of Christ.

"... Love therefore is the fulfillment of the law" (Rom. 13:10).

The greatest of faith, hope, and love, *is* love. The Greek definition of this word *love* is *charity* — which is exactly how the King James Version interprets this word. Charity is Christian love for God and men. This love comes from God. Therefore, a worthy action which does not stem from this love is not love at all.

As callous at it sounds, this is the unquestionable reading of Scripture. If I give all my possessions to the poor and give my body to be burned but do not have love, it "profits me nothing." If I know all mysteries, have all knowledge, have all faith — so as to remove mountains — and do not have love, "I am nothing."

Since God's plan for our life is an uncharted course, we must understand and apply the correct principles if we hope to walk down it. We can look inward to discover the talents and emotions which clue us to the "good works" God created us to do. But to figure out how to use these talents, we must be motivated out of love.

LOVE IS THE SET OF GLASSES WHICH WE MUST LOOK THROUGH TO BRING INTO FOCUS THE DIRECTION WE ARE TO HEAD.

If you do not have love, you cannot complete the course.

Through love we have *faith* (Gal. 5:6). Through love we *serve* one another (Gal. 5:13). We must *walk* in love (Eph. 5:2). We must *labor* in love (1 Thess. 1:3).

We must feed on love to understand where God is leading us.

". . . That you, being *rooted* and *grounded* in love, may be able to comprehend with all the saints what is the breadth and length and height and depth . . ." (Eph. 3:17-18).

Clearly, here, once we draw our strength and vision from love, God will give us comprehension as to how to use our talents for the Kingdom. That understanding — of the breadth, length, height, and depth — makes it possible to move down the course. Gain God's love and allow that love to show you how to use your talents.

The analogy here is that of a tree, being rooted and grounded in order to grow, for its leaves to sprout, for its fruit to spring forth.

"You will know them by their fruits," Jesus says in Matthew 7:16.

Notice that Jesus did not say, you will know them by their leaves, but by their fruits. What's the difference between a leaf and a fruit? A leaf makes a tree look beautiful and shows life. A fruit is something others can come and pluck off and eat.

Therefore Jesus is not interested in healthy-looking trees that are bedecked with beautiful leaves. Christians are sadly mistaken who take this Scripture to mean Christians who lead a godly lifestyle, avoid temptation, and shun all appearances of evil are bearing fruit. Such behavior shows life. But such behavior, alone, does not produce fruit.

Fruit is good works and nothing else. It's the ability to allow others to pluck something off of you and use it for his or her own nourishment, strength, and well-being.

This is not to speak negatively at all regarding the need to lead a righteous life. After all, fruit does not grow from a dead tree either. The point is, Jesus is not content with Christians who have life and bear beautiful leaves, but bear no fruit (good works) for others to enjoy. In fact, Jesus has commanded that trees which fail to bear fruit be cut down — this would include the dead ones as well as the live ones which fail to bear fruit.

"And seeing a lone fig tree by the road, He came to it, and found nothing on it except leaves only; and He said to it, 'No longer shall there ever be any fruit from you.' And at once the fig tree withered" (Matt. 21:19).

This may sound harsh, and perhaps even unacceptable to some. But keep in mind, before you were born God created "good works" for you to do. You were sent from God's hands to earth for the primary purpose of performing those "good works." If you are a Christian content with leading a righteous life, and think that is bearing fruit, you are misguided. Your righteous example is simply demonstrating life within you. And if that's all you have, you will eventually wither.

Fruit is that which allows others to receive the benefits of your God-given talents.

15

The Humble
Servant

Love shows you which fruit to bear. That way you don't offer your body to be burned when God has really called you to help the poor. In other words, God is not interested in just good works, but the *right* good works. He may have called someone else to give his body to be burned and called you to give your possessions to the poor. That's why Paul said it "profits me nothing" when acting without love.

When you look just for *acts* of love — instead of allowing love to control your acts — you are missing how God truly wants you to employ your good works.

You may think it's a high calling of love to counsel young gang members, but God may have called you to counsel the youth in your own church — or vice versa. Don't feel bad if God has given you a greater love for church youth than for gang youth. This is just one way in which God uses your emotions, and why you should learn to follow them correctly. God is perfectly capable of giving another Christian a heart which is more desirous to counsel gang members than church members.

Don't walk in someone else's calling — find your own.

Get love in your heart and then listen to God tell you how to use your talents. You'll make mistakes and won't always be right. But you'll always be trying. That's what counts. In time you'll make adjustments and discern the voice of God.

Like an infant, it's difficult to recognize what God is saying at first. But the infant keeps listening, keeps trying to understand, keeps trying to obey those parental words. Eventually, the child does understand.

So will you.

Once love bears fruit, you then have to serve it. This makes you a servant. Little is more destructive to a Christian's walk than to forget that he or she is a servant.

Much can be said about a servant's heart. Much can be said about the act of serving. But nothing can be said that is more important than having a humble heart while serving.

Without a humble heart you will *not* make

progress down God's path. You may be famous. You may have fortune. You may have much power. But, in God's eyes, you will be stuck in your tracks without a humble heart.

"And whoever exalts himself shall be humbled; and whoever humbles himself shall be exalted" (Matt. 23:12).

This Scripture is black and white, it needs no lengthy interpretation, it's cut and dried, it comes straight from the Lord's mouth.

Memorize it. Live by it. Trust it.

For such a short Scripture, this verse offers a powerful punch. It tells you how to get ahead. It tells you how to fail. It's a promise. It's simple to understand: exalt yourself and you will be humbled. Humble yourself and you will be exalted.

Personally, I believe this is the most important Scripture to "finish the course." Though I may not always use my talents skillfully, read my emotions correctly, love earnestly, or discern God's voice properly — if I humble myself, I will be exalted.

That's because our Lord's Scripture places no other conditions on being exalted. It may take you longer to get where you're going if you are not practicing the other principles, but you will eventually get there if you humble yourself.

I view this Scripture as a *law,* not a principle. It works for the believing and unbelieving alike. I've seen it happen. All those who humble themselves are exalted, and those who don't are humbled. Like the sun and rain, both the believing and unbelieving benefit from natural laws at work.

That's why this Scripture is placed in an "either/or" statement. Laws work this way, every time. Either the airplane is built aerodynamically or it will fall. Either you stop the bleeding or you will die. Either you water the plant or it will wither. These conditions are controlled by *natural laws*. They are immutable, they can't be broken without suffering *opposite* consequences.

This Scripture is phrased as any natural law would be: *Either* it's done correctly *or* you suffer the *opposite* consequences.

The word *humble* needs some clarification, however, because it means many things to many people — modest, abasement, insignificant, lowly, unassuming, not proud. In fact, it means all of these things.

But what do these words mean?

They mean striking a proper balance of self-worth, evaluation, and behavior. They mean *not* thinking more of yourself than who you really are. But they *don't* mean thinking and acting less than who you really are. This latter type of conduct is correctly called *false* humility. There's little difference between the fellow who thinks he knows it all than the fellow who acts like he knows nothing at all — both are useless.

A humble heart, like love, is not proven by acts. It's an attitude.

A humble man knows when to be assertive and when to take a step back; when to speak up and when to shut up; when to make a point and when it would be pointless to do so.

A humble man knows how to take criticism, how to lead, and how to follow.

A humble man understands that he knows some things but is ignorant in most things; understands that he has much to offer but his opinion may not always be in the offering; understands that he is made of dust but is still a child of God.

I've worked with scores of people — young and old alike — over the years. Only a handful of these people ever mastered humility. Most suffer from one, or more, connected problems. They think they are worth more than really they are; they can't take criticism; they get hurt when their opinion is not consulted or followed; they refuse to work diligently to improve their worth; they have no patience to climb the ladder; they have no idea how to act when overlooked; they refuse to have a servant's attitude; they want responsibility before learning responsibility.

Most important — and underscore this point — these people are there to promote themselves — not others, or the employer, or the business, or the overall goal.

In other words, they are proud, not humble. Their pride lowers their worth and usefulness in the business world. Employers are not looking to promote people who are going to pick a fight with them on any of these matters. The employer will look for the most qualified *humble* person — the learner; the self-starter; the person who knows what to say, when to say it, and when to take the lead; the person who's first interest is promoting the goal and others, rather than self.

Humility does not equal bashfulness, timidity, or passiveness.

The humble man, above all else, is a learner who knows when to take charge.

If you learn love, God will show you which fruit to produce; that is, how to use your talents to benefit mankind, how to complete the "good works" God chose you to do.

If you learn humility, you will learn how to excel, how to break down barriers that prevent you from excelling, and how to get those gifts into the hands of people who really need them.

If being *humble* is still a difficult concept to understand, follow this attitude:

Your purpose is to perform the good works you were created to do, and neither others — nor yourself — should ever stop you from completing that course. If you are in a position where people cannot pluck fruit off your tree, then assert some control over your life. If you are in a position where you are cramming your fruit down the throats of people who don't want it — for good reasons or for bad — then stop it.

16

Get Out
of the Boat

Knowing the ingredients and knowing the recipe does not make the cake. The cake needs a cook. Without a cook, the cake remains nothing but a heap of raw food components.

Talents and emotions are God's gifts to you — they are your ingredients. God's faith, love, and humble heart are your instructions for putting those ingredients together — they are your recipe.

But the final product — your calling in God — is dependent upon your effort, care, attention, time, work, vision, and determination. You are the cook.

Stepping out into the calling of God is *not* easy. It requires courage, risk taking, and confidence. You'll need commitment, thick skin, and ambition.

You'll be discouraged by others, confronted by mountains, and beset by confusion. Expect to feel pain, frustration, and hardship as well as fulfillment, accomplishment, and victory.

Stepping out in God is *not* a game — it's victory over Satan, and Satan is not going to make your challenge easy.

There is nothing in Scripture indicating that you are going to get a free and easy ride to God's destination. In fact, if you don't feel that your very survival is at stake at times, perhaps you're not traveling on God's path.

Everyone's life should be a journey from Capernaum to Bethsaida.

> And immediately He made the disciples get into the boat, and go ahead of Him to the other side, while He sent the multitudes away.
>
> And after He had sent the multitudes away, He went up to the mountain by Himself to pray; and when it was evening, He was there alone.
>
> But the boat was already many stadia away from the land, battered by the waves, for the wind was contrary.
>
> And in the fourth watch of the night He came to them, walking on the sea.

And when the disciples saw Him walking on the sea, they were frightened, saying, "It is a ghost." And they cried out for fear.

But immediately Jesus spoke to them saying, "Take courage, it is I; do not be afraid."

And Peter answered Him and said, "Lord, if it is You, command me to come to You on the water."

And He said, "Come!" And Peter got out of the boat, and walked on the water and came toward Jesus.

But seeing the wind, he became afraid, and beginning to sink, he cried out, saying, "Lord, save me!"

And immediately Jesus stretched out His hand and took hold of him, and said to him, "O you of little faith, why did you doubt?"

And when they got into the boat, the wind stopped (Matt. 14:22-34).

The boat is representative of the Church; the sea representative of the world. This incident is figurative of Christ's eventual leaving and Second Coming.

For the first time, the disciples were separated from Christ. That's why Jesus "made the disciples" get into the boat (the King James Version renders "constrained his disciples"). The disciples didn't want to leave their Lord.

While in the boat the wind (Satan) and the sea (the world) "battered" the boat, so much so that they were "straining at the oars" to make any progress at all (Mark 6:48). In other words, the Church would be persecuted and its progress continually hampered by Satan.

Jesus, seeing the disciples straining at the oars, came walking to them on the water. When the disciples saw Him, they were frightened, thinking He was a ghost. How often the Church tries to get where God is taking them all on their own — never even looking for Christ's miraculous powers to help them. It's so easy to forget that Jesus *is in the midst* of all the persecution and the attacks by Satan.

When Peter saw the Lord walking on the water, he asked the Lord to "command" him to come to Him. Jesus said, "Come."

This is the point of this book: The willingness to get out of the boat (the Church) even during a frightening storm of rising waves and wind (the world and Satan) and walk in the world with your very future at stake.

For all those Christians who think the Lord has confined them to the Church, that they should never risk leaving the safer haven of the body of Christ, that they should never step out on their own — with great danger surrounding their every step — this is the Scripture to put that fallacy to rest.

Jesus said, "Come."

Only Peter got out of the boat. This, too, is typical. Only one of the 12 disciples had the courage, desire, ambition, faith, and determination to risk all to walk with Jesus OUT IN THE WORLD — where wind and wave threatened his very life.

Sure, the Church as a whole has a mission (the boat) but every individual also has a mission (Peter walking on the water). Both will be attacked. The Church is safer, having the whole body of Christ to lift one another up, to teach, train, exhort, and encourage. The Church is not a place to hide, however, its purpose is to raise up ambassadors to the world. But to be an ambassador, you've got to get out of the boat.

"Therefore, we are ambassadors for Christ . . ." (2 Cor. 5:20).

And being an ambassador has its risks.

"I am an ambassador in chains," the apostle Paul said (Eph. 6:20).

An ambassador is someone sent to a foreign government to be an official representative of his own government — in this case, the kingdom of God.

Every ambassador lives in the foreign country he is negotiating with to protect the interests of his own country. Sure, he gets all the support needed from his home country, but he cannot be an ambassador if he never gets out of the boat.

Being an ambassador in a foreign land is dangerous. American embassies are constantly under threat and attack around the world. Don't expect your ambassadorship to be any different. It wasn't easy for Peter when he got out of the boat.

Peter was actually walking on the water and against the wind before he became frightened. But when his faith sunk, so did he. Peter cried out, "Lord, save me!"

Immediately Jesus stretched out His hand and took hold of him.

Actually, it was good for us that Peter began to doubt, began to sink. For we know that anytime — as we walk on that water — we begin to lose faith we can shout, "Lord, save me," and immediately Jesus will stretch out His hand and rescue us. Jesus is *not* going to let us drown because we stepped out on faith. If need be, Christ will walk us back to the boat to renew our strength, faith, and trust.

If Peter had never doubted, perhaps we wouldn't know from this example that Jesus is always there ready to save us — and many of us would never take that chance.

You may know the ingredients and recipe to your destination in Christ, but these are worthless if *you* don't have the ambition or faith to step out on your own and become an ambassador for Christ.

17

Do Not Lean on Your Own Understanding

Sometimes when walking on God's path, you will not be absolutely sure you are going in the right direction. Sometimes this new direction could be very risky.

But I have this confidence — God will never punish me for *trying* to walk in the direction I think He is taking me. My decision may be wrong, but I'm fully assured that if I begin to sink, Christ will rescue me and put me back up on that water to start over again.

When I was fired from Moral Majority, and before I had another job, I went out and bought $8,000 worth of computer equipment. To this day, I don't know how I got the loan for all this equipment. I felt I needed it, though. I felt that if I had the right tools, I could continue to write for the Lord in some capacity. Of course I had disbeliefs — thoughts that my decision was foolish. I knew I was risking much of what I owned if I defaulted.

I determined to trust God. To step out on the water. To risk what I did own in hopes that I was moving in the right direction. If not, I would pray that I would not be destroyed.

About six weeks later, I landed my freelance contract job to write fundraising letters. As a freelancer, I had to use my own equipment. By having my own equipment, I then learned how to help raise funds for worthy causes. This same equipment was later used to start the Christian Action Network.

Thank God I made the right decision. But for all those who think they have to be 100 percent sure in their decision and faith before stepping out in God, you're wrong.

The Gospel of Luke relates the story of a father who brought his demon-possessed, mute son to Jesus to be delivered (Mark 9:17-27).

The father said to the Lord, "And it often throws him both into the fire and into the water to destroy him. But if you can do anything, take pity on us and help us!"

Jesus responded, "If you can! All things are

possible to him who believes."

The boy's father responded, "I do believe, help me in my unbelief" (Mark 9:22-24).

What a contradicting statement! I do believe, help me in my unbelief. Is it really possible to have both belief and unbelief at the same time? Clearly the answer is yes. Will Christ honor such mixed faith? He did with the father of this demoniac son.

I find faith to be relative to risk — the greater the risk, the more unbelief mixed with belief.

It was much easier to have 100 percent faith when I was younger — and didn't own a car, a home, and have a wife and four children to support. Now every risky decision is not just a bed I will make for myself, but a bed I will make for five other people as well.

That's tougher. No doubt Satan's fiery darts start piercing you in the head — raising questions and doubts — when deciding to go forward. You can't help, when making a decision that affects your entire family, to carefully review the consequences of your decisions — and the disastrous results that could come if you're wrong.

When I started the Christian Action Network, I did so on just $75. I still remember telling my wife, after I quit my job at Richard Delgaudio and Associates, that I wasn't going to look for another job, that I was going to start my own Christian activist organization.

She was not comfortable with the decision, though she displayed great patience. This decision — the biggest I ever made in my life — would surely result in complete disaster if wrong.

I questioned whether such a leap of faith was a responsible action for a husband and a father. I am supposed to provide security for my family — direction, support, and leadership. Here I was, not only refusing to look for another job, but using the last bit of our finances to start an activist organization.

Did I have doubts? Many. Did I have anxiety, worry, and unbelief? You bet. But I had enough faith to move forward — and it was enough.

I believed God was speaking to me and telling me to start the Christian Action Network. But my heart alone wasn't enough assurance to make that final decision. I had to look at all that God had done with my life up to that point to get the final answer.

I was a writer. I was a good communicator. I could raise money — I had proved it for many organizations. I had a heart to confront the major moral and social issues destroying America. Because of my six years as editor of the *Moral Majority Report,* I probably knew the issues as well as anyone in America.

But there were no activist organizations for me to work with which needed the talents, knowledge, and skills I had to offer. I was in a bind to make a decision to change my career completely or start my own organization.

My heart told me to start the Christian Action Network. My experiences told me to start the Christian Action Network. It made some sense, but was it really God, or just my own personal wants and desires? I honestly never knew for sure.

So I went with the "leading indicators." I looked

at the ingredients that God so patiently put within me and developed. I prayed and listened much and heard God say, "Start it."

I desperately wanted to be 100 percent sure — to know beyond any doubt or unbelief. I prayed for stronger faith, more confidence, more trust. But I had all I was going to get. It was up to me to get out of the boat and walk on that water.

I told the Lord, "I do believe, help me in my unbelief."

With $75 I sent letters to 200 people to help me get this organization started. Five donors came back. With the funds that came back, I mailed another 260 letters. And with those funds, I mailed letters to 300 more people. So it went until I mailed a total of 3,000 letters.

I took the results of those 3,000 mailings to two businessmen. After reviewing the responses they agreed to help back me financially, but under one condition: that I not draw a salary — not one penny — from the new organization.

It would be at least one year before I could personally draw a salary from the Christian Action Network, and then not much. What a risk! How would I ever live?

God blessed the organization and it grew. The results of my efforts clearly indicated that I moved in the direction God was leading me. To survive personally, God provided freelance writing jobs. I had to work tirelessly to do both.

The Christian Action Network is now three

years old. From those five donors, CAN has grown to 71,000 members strong. The tremendous achievements of this organization is a success story all in itself.

From "Larry King Live" to "Sonya Live," from CNN news to CBN news, from PBS's Bill Moyers to CBS's Mike Wallace — the Christian Action Network has gained notoriety for its accomplishments.

It *all* started — not on complete faith — but belief mixed with unbelief. I now have complete faith, because God helped me in my unbelief. It didn't happen overnight, but it did happen.

You are human. God knows that. God understands the struggle of moving out when all logic, common sense, and responsible actions tell you not to. God understands that you are under the fiery gun of Satan's darts when you do consider moving out.

Just remember that moving out in God doesn't always align itself with logic, common sense, and responsible actions. Therefore, if you make your decision not to move based on these factors alone, you are acting on unbelief.

This Scripture was most inspiring to me in making that decision to move forward: "Trust in the Lord with all your heart, and do not lean on your own understanding. In all your ways acknowledge Him, and He will make your paths straight" (Prov. 3:5-6).

Do not *lean* on your own understanding. What happens when you lean against something? You fall when it falls. Lack of understanding produces lack of faith. If you're leaning against it, as it tilts so will your faith.

In all your ways acknowledge Him and He will make your paths straight. If you acknowledge God in all your ways — even if you make the wrong decision — He will turn that decision into a straight path where He is leading you.

But you have to trust Him — trust Him against your understanding, and trust that He will straighten your path if a wrong decision is made.

It would be against the nature of God — and all that we know about Him in the Bible — to punish you for taking a step of faith in the wrong direction.

Press onward and forget what lies behind.

"Brethren, I do not regard myself as having laid hold of it yet; but one thing I do: forgetting what lies behind and reaching forward to what lies ahead.

"I press on toward the goal for the prize of the upward call of God in Christ Jesus" (Phil. 3:13-14).

The apostle Paul admits that he is not perfect — such an admission is also a confession that mistakes have been made. But he knows that to finish the course, to reach the calling for which God created him, he'd have to press on and forget the past.

"Not that I have already obtained it, or have already become perfect, but I press on in order that I may lay hold of that for which also I was laid hold of by Christ Jesus" (Phil. 3:12).

18

Wrestling with God

Hold God to His promises. Struggle with God, wrestle with Him, contend with Him. Hold God to His Word and don't let go.

I know this will be a difficult concept for some, if not most, Christians. The mere thought that you would have to grapple with God to get what He has already promised sounds absurd — perhaps irreverent.

If you're surprised, taken aback somewhat, remember — so was Jacob.

Jacob labored under Laban for 20 years in Paddan-aram before God told him, "Return to the land of your fathers and to your relatives, and I will be with you" (Gen. 31:3).

Herein lies both a command and a promise: Return to Canaan (a command) and I will be with you (a promise).

Perhaps the last thing Jacob expected was to find himself in a wrestling match with God on the journey home.

> Then Jacob was left alone, and a man wrestled with him until daybreak.
>
> And when he saw that he had not prevailed against him, he touched the socket of his thigh, so the socket of Jacob's thigh was dislocated while he wrestled with him.
>
> Then he said, "Let me go, for the dawn is breaking." But he said, "I will not let you go unless you bless me."
>
> So he said to him, "What is your name?" And he said, "Jacob."
>
> And he said, "Your name shall no longer be Jacob, but Israel; for you have striven with God and with men and have prevailed" (Gen. 32:24-28).

Jacob was commanded to return home, and God sent an angel to directly oppose his entrance back into the land which he was called.

This sounds contradictory, though not completely unusual for God. After all, God did promise Abraham that his descendants would rise through Isaac, then God commanded Abraham to sacrifice Isaac.

The fact that God called Jacob to return home and then sent an angel to stop him is no different of a parallel in Scripture. God was looking for something in Jacob, just like He was looking for something in Abraham.

In Abraham, God was looking for complete obedience even when God's commands made no logical sense, even when God's commands are counter to His promises.

What was God looking for in Jacob?

In Hosea we learn that Jacob's wrestling match with God was considered an act of maturity.

"In the womb he took his brother by the heel, and in his maturity he contended with God. Yes, he wrestled with the angel and prevailed. He wept and sought His favor" (Hos. 12:3-4).

In his maturity, Jacob contended with God. In his maturity, Jacob had to wrestle with God to get where he was going. So important is this principle, that God changed Jacob's name — and the name of a nation of people to follow — to Israel.

Israel means, "He who strives with God."

Sometime during your calling in God, you will struggle with God. You will receive the promise to "go forth," then God, himself, will try to stop you.

Whether you engage in the struggle and *prevail* will determine whether you, too, will receive God's blessing, as did Jacob. The willingness and ability to contend with God is a sign of maturity.

God wants to give His promises to you. But God is sifting out the pretenders from the contenders. God is looking for character — people who have fire in their heart to "finish the course." Nothing exposes that fire more than wrestling with God himself.

A wrestling match with God reveals diligence, desire, strength, ambition, courage, perseverance, and faithfulness — all the qualities of a mature man.

God is not going to let Christians waltz into the promises of God. God is going to turn the heat up and refine you into a mature man or woman. The same qualities needed to prevail against God will be needed to prevail against the world. If you can't prevail against God, then God is not going to thrust you into a position of prevailing against worldly forces. So you are tested — even as Jacob was tested before meeting Esau on that return trip home — to see if you have the maturity to receive God's calling.

This wrestling match is there to protect you — to keep you from being put in a position of defeat. Better to be defeated by God than by the world.

Jacob was scheduled to meet Esau — his brother whom he supplanted twice, his brother who vowed to kill him — the day after his wrestling match with God.

If Jacob would have lost his bout with God, he would not have entered into the promise of God — returning to his home — and he would not have to meet his brother, Esau. Jacob would have been spared this worldly confrontation. Jacob was tested to determine his readiness to enter into the promise.

The Bible is your resource in wrestling with God. In it are thousands of pledges God gave you. These pledges bind God to helping you in your hour of need.

Know them. Use them. Claim them. Hold God to His Word. Stand in there and fight. Prevail and win God's blessings. Don't cower.

When I founded the Christian Action Network I was without pay for one year. CAN was more than a full-time job. Therefore, I couldn't get a part-time job to receive income. Even if I did, it wouldn't be enough to support my family.

I was in a bind. CAN was blasting off, but I had no money to live on and keep my family going.

I wrestled with God. Clearly, my wrestling was with God, not Satan. I never thought it was Satan's fault that I didn't receive income from CAN. Neither was it any man's fault. This was simply a situation where God called and I answered, but the calling fell short of meeting my most basic needs — money to live on.

I knew God was testing me, to see if I would prevail in this wrestling match. At any time, God could have overwhelmingly blessed CAN so I could receive income. God chose not to in order to test me, to see if I would stand in there and contend with Him.

I found this Scripture to wrestle God with:

> Do not be anxious then, saying, "What shall we eat?" or "What shall we drink?" or "With what shall we clothe ourselves?"
>
> For all these things the Gentiles eagerly seek; for your heavenly Father knows that you need all these things.
>
> But seek first His kingdom and

His righteousness; and all these things
shall be added to you (Matt. 6:31-33).

This Scripture clearly indicates that when pursuing the kingdom of God you may be thrust into a position where you don't know how you're going to eat, drink, or clothe yourself. That was my position.

I determined to stand in there and not be the one to prove God's word can't be trusted. I decided that if God's word can't be trusted, then God would have to show me by failing to back His pledge: "All these things shall be added to you."

For that entire year God supplied me with various freelance writing jobs to supply my needs. There's only one way to prevail against God — by using His very own words.

But there have been many other bouts with God.

After I got my first writing job with the religious news service, something very odd happened. I couldn't write.

Writing had always been a natural talent for me. I hardly had to even think about it. The words just flowed out in a rational, orderly, and logical fashion — until I got my first job as a writer. Then I couldn't write a complete sentence that made sense. It was more than writer's block — it was writer's death.

I would take three to five hours just to write the lead paragraph to a news story. I knew what happened — God took the gift of writing from me. A grade-school child had a better chance of stringing together a news story than I had.

Here God called me to be a writer and opened the door, then He took all my writing abilities away from me. That made no sense. I was in a struggle with God, himself, to return my writing talents to me.

I stood in there, writing the best I could. Bit by bit, God gave me my skills back. But I had to *learn* to write. No longer was it a free and easy ride. I sweated with every news story. I prayed continuously for God to show me how to write if, indeed, He was going to take the gift from me.

God did. I *learned* to write. God walked me through, word by word, sentence by sentence, paragraph by paragraph, on how to write. It proved to be a fortunate experience to go through.

First, it made me a better writer. Now I can combine my gift with my knowledge of writing to make me a better writer.

Second, little did I know that several years later I would be working with scores of young, inexperienced writers at the *Moral Majority Report*. Because I had to *learn* to write, I could teach these young reporters what they needed to know. Without that experience, the best I could offer these reporters is, "I don't know what to tell you, it's a gift."

This was a wrestling match I needed to go through before entering the promise, or I wouldn't have been a very efficient editor at all.

A wrestling match with God is typically easy to distinguish. It's some obstacle that keeps you from reaching God's calling, but is clearly not the result of Satan's opposition.

Your strength is drawn from the Bible. For every struggle, there is a scriptural pledge that binds God to pull you through. I think all wrestling matches test your perseverance and diligence. Therefore, this is what God is looking for before He allows you to enter His promise.

"The precious possession of a man *is* diligence" [emphasis added] (Prov. 12:27).

Receiving a promise is a promotion in God's eyes. Only the diligent ever walk in that promise.

19

The Diligent Hand

Diligence: The steady, earnest, painstaking, and energetic effort to achieve something. It's the precious possession of man.

The diligent man never gives up, never caves in, never stops trying. The diligent man knows how to bounce back, how to scale mountains, how to keep moving.

Without diligence, a man becomes battered and worn, wearied and frustrated, hopeless and feeble.

Diligence is not just a quality or a character, it is power. Read closely the following Proverbs on the power of being diligent:

The hand of the diligent makes rich (Prov. 10:4).

The hand of the diligent shall rule (Prov. 12:24).

The soul of the diligent is made fat (Prov. 13:4).

The plans of the diligent lead surely to advantage (Prov. 21:5).

Up to this point, little has been said about the need to put forth the necessary effort to succeed in God's calling. Knowing the principles, practices, and concepts to success is required, but unless these are applied with diligence, they are mostly worthless.

Diligence leaves no room for excuses, laziness, or incompetence. The diligent man knows opportunity doesn't come seeking him, rather it is up to him to continue to ask, seek, and knock until opportunity is realized.

"Ask, and it shall be given to you; seek, and you shall find; knock, and it shall be opened to you" (Matt. 7:7).

Literally, the translation reads "keep asking, keep seeking, keep knocking." In other words, answers, opportunities, and open doors come to those who are diligent in their efforts.

Why doesn't God answer after the first effort? I have my own speculations. I believe that, being human, we couldn't possibly understand the answers of God at the start. We will make mistakes, get misdirected, and run into obstacles. Therefore, we need to keep asking, seeking, and knocking or we will never find the answers.

The diligent man knows that God wants to take him to his calling in God. With this confidence and trust, the diligent man never rests until he finds those answers.

I knew from the outset of my writing career that I had many disadvantages and handicaps — most having been previously reviewed. I realized that I was in competition with writers who had better backgrounds, education, training, and experience. Diligence was my answer to gaining advantage.

I became a Washington news correspondent for *Moody Monthly* (a 300,000 circulation Christian publication) because I wrote news stories no one else would touch for the money. For example, I wrote a story on the growing population of Muslim inmates in American prisons. It required much research and visits to prisons. I probably made about $1 an hour by the time the story was finished. I also wrote a news story on the growing popularity of the Ku Klux Klan under the Jimmy Carter administration. Few writers wanted to go into this hotbed of hate to write a news story.

When Moral Majority formed and released its national newspaper, the *Moral Majority Report*, I desperately wanted to be a part of this publication. It was well-funded and was not afraid of addressing social political issues (unlike most Christian publications at that time).

I asked the executive director of Moral Majority,

Dr. Ronald Godwin, whether I could go to Bloomington, Indiana, to write a story about a Mongoloid baby who was starved to death by medical personnel. I told him I had a hunch something was greatly amiss about the whole public story.

Dr. Godwin agreed to give me $50 a day (for travel, food, motel expenses, *and* pay) to crack the story if I could. Not a lot of money, for sure. But an opportunity, nevertheless.

I did crack the so-called "Baby Doe" case in Bloomington, but that's another story.

Several weeks after my return, Dr. Godwin ask me to take the job as editor of the newspaper. He told me, "We need someone who can look Satan in the face and not be afraid to ask questions." I made a name for myself in Christian journalism by going where no other Christian journalist dared to go.

I used the same diligence to write my first book, *Silent Shame: The Alarming Rise of Child Sexual Abuse* (Crossways Books, 1987). As far as I knew, no one but I wanted to go into prisons to interview child sexual offenders, read their strategies, and uncover their network. In other words, if a publisher wanted a book on how parents could protect their children from the hands of sex offenders, they'd have to get it from me. The publisher could look for a bigger name, more experienced writer, more reputable author, but I was the only one with the book.

Diligence: The steady, earnest, painstaking, and energetic effort to achieve something.

Diligence knows no fear, no hurt, no rejection.

Diligence never considers the negative, but only the possibilities. Diligence laughs at those who say, "It can't be done. You're wasting your time. You're not qualified."

Diligence makes people believe in you . . . and you in yourself. Diligence is power of the mind. It's the positive knowledge that it's not a question of *whether* but when.

I found that the more sure I am in my decision, the easier it is — not only to convince others — but to get others to help you. People ride on your confidence, or jump off because of the lack of your certainty. People want to associate themselves with winners, not those who think they may lose.

When I am convinced that I'm going to make something happen, and I need help from others, my mental approach is this: "Here's what I'm going to do. Now you can either jump on and help, or I'll do it without you." I never leave open the question that it can't be done without them. That's just plain nonsense. And those from whom you are seeking help know this. If they perceive in you that they are needed to accomplish a particular feat, they will probably be reluctant to help you. These people want to be absolutely convinced before helping you that you are absolutely convinced that it's going to get done with or without them.

Diligence: It's the power to persuade others, to bring them on your team.

Rarely will you get anywhere in your goals if you don't ask, or refuse, the help of others. These "others" are typically people successful in their own right. They already know what character of person it takes to be successful. If they don't see diligence in you, they will probably run — no matter how good your idea or your offer.

The diligent man never takes "no" for an answer. This doesn't mean he keeps bugging the same person over and over. But it does mean that a "no" answer from one person — or many — will not stop him. Sooner or later he will find the person who says "yes."

Don't take "no" as some sort of sign from God to stop. Don't take a slammed door or denial of opportunity as a sign from God. God's already told you to keep asking, keep seeking, and keep knocking.

Don't try to figure out why obvious doors remain shut, because the diligent man only knows to go to the next door. As you become successful, you will find many of those formerly shut doors are now opening to you.

Your true enemies are not the people who seemingly have the power to stop you. Your true enemies are found within you — discouragement, hurt feelings, laziness, self pity, withdrawal, pessimism, and dejection.

Here is the perfect example of the true enemy being within your heart and soul. The Lord spoke to Moses in Numbers 13 and commanded him to send out spies into the land of Canaan. Moses chose two men from each of the 12 tribes of Israel. After 40 days, the men returned and reported that the land "certainly does flow with milk and honey." The promises of God were both good and rewarding — if it could be taken.

But the men added, "We are not able to go up against the people, for they are too strong for us. . . .The land through which we have gone, in spying it out, is a land that devours its inhabitants, and all the people whom we saw in it are men of great size . . . we became like grasshoppers in our own sight, and so we were in their sight."

Two men, Joshua and Caleb, gave a different report: "We should by all means go up and take possession of it, for we shall surely overcome it."

An angry God responded by forbidding all Israelites from 20 years and upward from ever walking into the Promised Land. God was not about to send a band of negative, pessimistic, and discouraged people into a land that required great optimism and diligence.

We all know the outcome — the Israelites conquered the land of Canaan.

This is a lesson for you in *your* walk into God's Promised Land and calling.

The true enemies are not the giants who are there to devour you — and indeed they will if you let them. The true enemy is within yourself — the unwillingness to try, to fight, to conquer, to be diligent.

The diligent will rule — because they have the character to make it happen.

20

Shine before Men

"You are the light of the world" (Matt. 5:14).

The world not only includes the unbelieving — but its government, institutions, industries, culture, as well as its people. The world is all that which is outside the Church — education, entertainment, news media, medicine, business, science, and more.

The purpose of light is to expose darkness — all darkness. Light is truth. Darkness is falsehood. The purpose of light is *not* simply to bring the unbelieving into the fold of believers. For then the world is left just as dark as it formally was. The Church has gained a beam of light — but that light is then placed under a bushel (Matt. 5:15).

The good works you were created to do *is* light for the world to see. Accordingly then, believers receive their training, upbringing, education, and encouragement from the Church and then take their good works into the world for all to see as light.

"Let your *light* shine before men in such a way that they may see your *good works,* and glorify your Father who is in heaven" [emphasis added] (Matt. 5:16).

This Scripture mandates all of us to be ministers. The pastor was never intended to be propped up as the sole minister of a church. All believers are ministers. The pastor is a minister to the believing. The congregation is a minister to the world. The pastor uses his good works — the talents and abilities God has given him — to encourage, inspire, train, and reprove the congregation. The purpose of all this ministering is for us to then "go forth" into all the world — and not for the sole purpose of converting unbelievers into believers.

The Church is the pillar and support of truth (1 Tim. 3:15). What is the Church propping up as a pillar and support? The Church is not propping up itself — but the world. When the Church stops being the pillar and support of truth, the world will collapse accordingly.

We are already seeing it happening. Truth has fallen in the United States and so has its culture, freedoms, liberties, institutions, and more.

It's clear why. Christians, as a whole, have walked *out* of the world. We have walked out of the very world to which we were called to be a light, to be a pillar and support of truth, and to display the fruit of our good works. When Christians walked out a vacuum was created — a vacuum that sucked in humanists, secularists, atheists, antagonists, and more. Now, most of our institutions are run by those who hate the traditions, values, morals, religion, and truths of our Father. Even churches have not escaped the far-reaching tentacles of these enemies of truth.

We have only ourselves to blame. Our founding fathers tried to bring truth into every sector of this country. But we squandered our great heritage by dropping out of the world and turning it over to enemies of the truth.

Now our institutions, which affect our very lives, are in command by antagonists to the faith.

Every day, for the past 15 years, I've spent my life trying to restore truth to our nation. But I can tell you, we have very few friends who still stand for truth.

This book will not examine the great destruction these antagonists and revisionists have exacted on our society. That information will be revealed later. But I'm sure it has not escaped the eyes of most Christians that our society is falling apart.

All these evils have soared in the United States during the past 30 years: divorce, abortion, murder, illicit drug use, crimes of every sort, unwed pregnancies, child sexual abuse, family violence, scandal, runaways, kidnappings, homosexuality, and more.

As Christians, we have little or no say in the entertainment business, courts, laws, schools, media, colleges, government, culture, medicine, science, or scholastic thought.

Now our abandonment is costing us dearly. Where, at first, Christians decided to drop out of the world — under a misguided interpretation of Scripture to be separated from the world — we are now being persecuted by the enemies of the faith.

Our children can't pray in the public schools, government funds blasphemous attacks on our Christian faith, citizens can't erect nativity scenes on public property, ministers have been arrested for street preaching, Christian day-schools and home-schools have come under the strong arm of government agencies, school children now have to learn the "value" of alternative lifestyles — including homosexual conduct, and more.

Recently, I was called by a newspaper reporter who was working on an article about Christian revolt. This reporter said he spoke with many "fundamentalist" Christians who were arming themselves — with heavy weapons — to oppose any further state encroachment on their religious lifestyle.

What did these Christians think was going to happen when we stopped being the light to society, when we failed to be the pillar and support of God's truth, when we refused to "finish the course" by employing the good works God gave us? Did we really think the state would leave us alone? How sad . . . how utterly and painfully sad.

As a nation we don't need to worry about outside conquest. We will destroy ourselves. The enemy is within.

The news reporter went on to tell me that his primary coverage is as a "police beat" reporter. He told me of the escalating violence he has seen and its tragedy. I asked him why he thought this was so. His answer was so simple, so truthful, so stark: "The breakdown of the family." It sent chills down my spine. But he quickly added: "Of course, I can't say that. It's politically incorrect."

Exactly! What *needs* to be said is *not* being said. Christians have long been the defender of the family publicly, but our family institutions are still commandeered by anti-family proponents — those who think a family is whatever a person wants it to be. And it's killing our country — both figuratively and literally.

You and I can continue to watch the destruction of this nation from the sidelines if we want. God will give us that destruction if we choose it. If you think God will act differently, pick up any daily newspaper.

Here's a fundamental fact: WE ARE AT FAULT. We had the truth, but we kept it to ourselves. How selfish, how devastating, how anti-Christian.

As president of a Christian activist organization, I am in a fortunate position to look at our nation and determine where the wall is crumbling. On the one side of the wall is an ocean of enormous strength, pounding its waves steadily against the walls of tradition, truth, and righteousness. On the other side of the wall are a few Christians plugging the leaks and bracing the wall. But the wall is old, void of strength, and crumbling within. The wall will fall unless we revive the stones and mortar. We can't continue to plug it much longer.

The Church needs to get out of its buildings and infiltrate the world — to become the ambassadors we were called to be, to strengthen the wall of truth by being the bricks and mortars that it is made from. Let me make it more clear: Christians need to be the teachers, professors, the family thearpists, the politicians, entertainers, book writers, journalists, owners of businesses, the doctors, scientists, pyschiatrists, and the scholars. You can take your place in the world — accept your ambassadorship — without becoming a part of the world. You are such a vital part to the survival of this nation. The good works God gave you is not just for other Christians, but for *all* the world.

Christ, himself, called your good works *light.* And He has commanded you to present your light for all the world to see.

"You are the light of the world. A city set on a hill cannot be hidden" (Matt. 5:14).

Read this Scripture carefully. You (the Church, which includes you) are the light of the world. The Church is a city and it *cannot* be hidden. Hidden from who? From other Christians? No. It cannot be hidden from the world.

You are a minister. You are in the ministry. Get your strength, upbringing, training, and encouragement from the Church and then get out into the world and be that beam of light.

Without it, our world will crumble.

21

The Finishing Line

Perhaps the hardest part of "finishing the course" is that period where you have no choice but to wait for God to work His mighty hand.

There will come times when — even after following every detail of this book, saying every prayer that can be said, and making every effort that can be made — all you can do is wait. The Israelites had to wait for God all along their trip in the wilderness. They waited for manna every day, water at various times, and other miracles — such as the parting of the Red Sea — just to survive. And they grumbled because they knew they had done all they could, but it wasn't enough. They still had to wait for God to provide the missing elements.

Waiting *is* a part of faith: "Wait for the Lord; be strong, and let your heart take courage; yes, wait for the Lord" (Ps. 27:14).

I had several examples of "waiting" on the Lord I wanted to relate in this chapter. But nothing was more powerful than what happened to me after finishing this book.

It was just before Thanksgiving. This book was already at the publisher's, a contract was in the offing, and the galleys were being set. I told New Leaf Press that I wanted to write a concluding chapter, something that would sum up the principles in this book.

Meanwhile, as negotiations were taking place, my son Michael, 11, was complaining of a pain on the right side of his pelvis. The doctor said it was nothing but a pulled muscle. Yet, after several weeks the pain got worse. It didn't help that he fell down while sleigh riding, and once while walking down the steps. Logically, these mishaps explained why the pain was becoming more intense. But something inside me told a different story — that his condition was not a pulled muscle.

My wife, Bonnie, took Michael back to the doctor, but the x-rays proved negative. He was then scheduled for an MRI (a device that uses sound waves to photograph internal organs).

We had an appointment with an orthopedic surgeon to go over the MRI results a few days later. However, it was quickly moved up after the doctor received the film.

"Michael has a tumor," the doctor said in the

examination room. Michael was standing nearby, but didn't seem to understand the significance of the diagnosis. Bonnie and I looked at each other, both to see how the other was handling the information. By appearances we took the first blow well.

"What does this mean?" I asked.

"It means you need to select a medical center to put Michael into so he can get treated."

"What are they going to do to him?" I came back.

"Well, they may have to do surgery to remove it, or give him chemotherapy or radiation."

It was the word "chemotherapy" that began to crush me. In a roundabout way, the doctor was telling me the tumor was cancerous. I excused Bonnie and Michael so I could talk privately with the doctor. A nurse stayed in the room in case I broke down or suffered something worse.

He began, "I didn't know how much to say with Michael in the room, but it looks like the tumor is malignant."

"Can it be treated?" I struggled to ask.

"Well," he said, sitting relaxed on an examination table, "if it was on his arm or foot, we could amputate. But being on his pelvis — well, we can't amputate his pelvis."

His words sounded harsh, insensitive.

"Is it always fatal?" I asked.

"No, not always. Ten years ago there wouldn't be much hope. But oncology (the study of tumors) has come a long way during the past decade."

He was then silent, looking perhaps like he was

being bothered with so many questions. I thanked him and left.

What the doctor wrote in his report was that Michael probably had Ewings sarcoma — a deadly form of cancer that had very unfavorable results when located on the pelvis, or, as the doctor had told me, when the tumor cannot be amputated. Michael wasn't scheduled for a biopsy until almost two weeks later. Even then, it would take another week to get the final results back.

For the next two weeks Bonnie and I waited. The news that came forth during that time offered no hope. Not only had the orthopedic doctor diagnosed the tumor as Ewings, so did two radiologists. We were told by experts, confidentially, that radiologists were rarely wrong on such diagnoses.

One cannot imagine all the things that run through the mind when a child has been diagnosed with a terminal disease. My wife and I had three other children at home — should we tell them? What should I tell Michael? Should I wait until a conclusive diagnosis had been reported, and then tell him? Why would God take our only son? How much pain will he go through? How will he handle it? How will I or my wife or my other children handle it? How long will it take?

The doctors examining Michael would offer no answers. Rightfully so, until a firm diagnosis was in hand, they weren't about to speculate on his future. I didn't blame them. The possibilities of what Michael would go through were endless depending on the condition of the tumor, its size, whether it had spread, and endless other factors.

So we waited. I hit my lowest point when Michael was having to undergo a bone scan. During this procedure Michael was given an injection of radiation that infiltrated his bones. He then laid under a special kind of x-ray machine that photographed every bone in his body. I sat in a hard, fiberglass chair watching the procedure. From my viewpoint I could see what the lab technicians were watching, a computer image that slowly captured his bone structure on screen. It seemed like ten agonizing minutes would pass before each picture was fully developed on screen.

I watched, hoping and praying, that no additional tumors would appear on his brain, lungs, or other vital organs. I became lightheaded because each image developed so slowly. It didn't help that although I could see what was appearing on screen, I only had a vague idea what the technicians were examining. I saw growth marks, which were similar in nature to the tumor, on every joint of his body. This I reasoned, was natural since his bones would still be growing around these areas. But how was I to know for sure? No one in the lab would give me a thumbs up or thumbs down on anything they saw. When they were finished, they simply sent Michael and I on our way.

More waiting. More not knowing.

I did everything I could to continue to run a business and keep up the spirits of my family. I decided to tell my oldest daughter Melissa, 14, what was happening because I wanted her to go out of her way to help her mother with whatever chores needed to be done.

She cried, but then performed like a little miracle worker.

Personally, I thought I might not survive it all. I had to stay strong at a time when my heart felt like putty. And I hated waiting. I wanted to do something to help Michael, to take the pain and tumor away. As a parent, I couldn't help but feel tremendous guilt that there was nothing I could do. In times past when he got hurt or ran into trouble, there was always something I could do to make him better. But now, nothing.

I was totally at the mercy of God. Then I remembered what I always did in the past when I did all that I could do and then had to wait for God. I held God to His words and promises.

I asked God to tell me whether Michael was going to die or not. If he was going to die, then give me the peace, the strength, and the ability to go through this tragedy. But if Michael wasn't going to die, then allow me to pray for his healing.

"Just tell me, God," I prayed. "Tell me whether he's going to die or not. You already know, so tell *me*. Tell me whether to encourage my family to have faith that he will be healed, or tell me whether to prepare my family for his death."

First, I tried accepting the fact that he would die. Then I tried drawing upon the strength of the Lord to carry me through. But I had no peace that he would die. Then I tried accepting the fact that God would heal him. There only, I found peace. And I'm fully confident that it wasn't wishful thinking that I was feeling.

Here was the fascinating realization that took

place in my mind and then in my heart: It is the nature of Christ to heal; that the New Testament is full of stories of healings, not death; and that it is rare that Christ refuses to heal. I couldn't think of a single instance when Christ denied a request for healing in Scripture. Therefore, I realized, Christ is more inclined to heal Michael than to allow him to die. Sure, God allows children to die. In fact, my sister died of leukemia when she was two years old — no matter how hard my father prayed. So this, I clearly understood. Nevertheless, it is within the nature of Christ to heal. And here, the Scriptures were absolutely clear.

Please understand, at first, I didn't pray that Michael be healed. At first, I simply prayed that God tell me whether or not Michael was going to die or be healed. I believed that God told me that He wanted to heal Michael, that this was within His will; because whenever I tried accepting God's decision to allow Michael to die, there was no peace.

So I prayed for God's healing. Throughout these prayers I was repeatedly given one bad diagnostic opinion after another regarding Ewings sarcoma, where the tumor was located, and the rate of survivability. Every medical forecast seemed to indicate Michael would die.

All I could do was wait and hold God to His Word. Then God gave me a Scripture. "Pleasant words are a honeycomb, sweet to the soul and healing to the bones" (Prov. 16:24).

Here was something I could do. I could give Michael nothing but pleasant words, because my Bible said it was healing to the bones.

Meanwhile, I also prepared Bonnie and myself in case I was wrong. (Please note my belief mixed with unbelief as I pointed out earlier.) I did this by not focusing so much on what was happening to Michael, since there was little I could do, and instead focusing on God's will. God, I knew, loved Michael more than I. If it was God's will to have Michael be with Him, then I would accept that decision.

There is no human explanation I can offer to explain the peace that surrounded Bonnie and me on the day of Michael's biopsy. There is no logical rationale that can explain why I believed Michael was going to live, but had complete peace if the doctors said he was going to die. It was God who showered His love on Bonnie and me so tremendously that it would be impossible to understand mentally.

Rather than being nervous wrecks as the minutes were closing in on being informed of the fate of our son, we were swept away by the power of God's love. The operation should have been over in an hour and a half, but it wasn't. There was a problem, though we were given no details. The procedure would take longer than expected, we were told. All kinds of things threatened to run through our minds. And if a needle dropped unexpectedly, both Bonnie and I would probably have leaped out of our chairs. But peace and joy were still with us.

About 45 minutes later we received a call in the surgery waiting room. It was the surgeon. The initial results of the biopsy proved negative for cancer. The tumor was probably benign. Furthermore, the surgeon said, the delay was caused by having trouble even finding the tumor. It was so much smaller than what the MRI indicated that they had to take another x-ray to make sure they were in the right spot! However, he cautioned us from getting too excited until the tissue sample grew in the lab for a week. Only when the final results were in, he said, would we know for sure.

Somehow, I knew for sure. A week later when the lab tests were finished, the tumor still proved benign. Currently, our son is finishing treatment with steroids which are drying up the remaining parts of the tumor.

Waiting on the Lord is perhaps the hardest part of "finishing the course." It takes place when you've done all that you can do — when you are left with nothing but the promises of God, your faith, and the peace God gives you that He will finish what needs to be done.

It's easy to forget, I assure you, that though God wants you to be ambitious, to be diligent, to use your talents, to make the best of every opportunity, to use your emotions and your love and your humble heart to take you down His paths, that He still wants you to know that it is He who is the final author of the turning points in your destiny.

Don't wait when you should be moving. I can't emphasize this enough. If you haven't done all that is outlined in this book, then God is still waiting on YOU!

But once you have completed all that you can do, then wait on the Lord — seek His peace, hold fast to His words, guard your faith, and allow God to open the door.

Once again, I must ask you: Are you a doer or a reader? I revealed many exciting but also painful and even humiliating moments in my life for the sole purpose of letting you know that no matter where you came from, no matter what your education, no matter what your social class or manners, no matter what the obstacles are, you *can* "finish the course."

Get out of the boat and walk with Christ!

If you would like to write Martin Mawyer or would like more information about Christian Action Network, please write to:

Christian Action Network
P.O. Box 606
Forest, VA 24551